BRISTOL AEROSPACE
SINCE 1910

BRISTOL AEROSPACE

SINCE 1910

GEOFF GREEN

First Published 1985

ISBN 0 9510519 0 3 (Hardback)

ISBN 0 9510519 1 1 (Softback)

Published by
Geoff Green,
37 Underhill Road,
Charfield,
Wotton-under-edge,
Glos. GL12 8TQ

Photoset and printed by
Printing and Graphic Services (Bristol) Limited,
Golf Course Lane,
Filton,
Bristol BS12 7QS

(Cover)
The Shuttleworth Trust's preserved Bristol Fighter *D8096* at Filton.

(Back Cover Upper)
Bristol Freighter *XJ470* in service with the Aircraft and Armaments Experimental Establishment, Boscombe Down.

(Back Cover Lower)
Bristol Bulldog *G-ABBB* at Filton in 1961.

(Frontispiece)
BRISTOL TYPE 142M BLENHEIM (1936)
***K7033*, the prototype Blenheim which first flew on 25 June 1936.** *(Flight photo)*

(Below)
CHANGING FACE OF FILTON -1
The former 'bus sheds in 1910/11 after the first extension.

Contents

Acknowledgements

As I wasn't born until 1944, and didn't take an active interest until many years later, it is impossible for me to have first hand knowledge of the entire lifespan of the Filton enterprise. Much that is written here therefore follows on from what has been recorded by former *Bristol* employees such as Clifford Tinson, Chris Barnes and the various past members of the Filton Press Office.

I must especially thank Mel West, Howard Berry, Sean Greene, the members of the Filton Photographic Department and Barry Rudrum.

Thanks are also due to Mike Fish, Mike Tozer, Jim Oughton, George Lambe, Jack Smith, Roy Drew, Peter Wedgewood, Duncan Greenman, Clive Leyman, Frank Crowfoot, Geoff Bruce, Dave Oyns, Allan Macfarlane, Frank Edwards, Carl Ralph, Phil Sposito, Sue Turner, John Heaven, John Hutchinson, Stanley Larkham, Terry Bickerton and Dave Bidder.

The following publications and publishers have been of assistance. *Flight, The Aeroplane,* Ian Allan Limited, Putnam.

All photographs courtesy of British Aerospace except where stated otherwise.

Introduction

Bristol will be remembered most for its important links with the sea but in the last 150 years other forms of transport have gained dominance. Almost every conceivable engineering artefact has been made in Bristol or its hinterland with some of the largest products becoming famous on rails, on land or in the air.

Railway locomotives will be recalled mostly by enthusiasts alone but Bristol 'buses and Bristol aeroplanes have had a greater impact on the everyday life of the average man and woman in the street.

Both of these famous enterprises were the product of the imagination of one man in the first instance. Neither one was built up for its curiosity or interest but owes its existence to a venture founded solely for the pursuit of personal gain. The capitalist ideals of the Victorian and Edwardian eras are not readily accepted in more enlightened times but many people are still reaping the benefits of empires created on a firm monetary foundation seventy-five or more years ago.

Born in Bristol on 10 March 1854 Sir George White was an entrepreneur in the best Victorian tradition, ''gifted with great natural shrewdness, prudent yet quick to seize an advantageous opening, doggedly pertinacious in pursuit of what he seemed right yet withal a generous opponent and appreciative employer''. The head of George White & Company of Bristol he was elected President of the Bristol Stock Exchange whilst still in his 'twenties.

His personality and monetary skills made him a millionaire but he was also a philanthropist to a degree. A benefactor of Bristol institutions, he was President and Treasurer of the Bristol Royal Infirmary and was instrumental in the building of the King Edward VII extension. One of the Charity Trustees, he was Governor of Bristol Grammar School amongst others and was interested in the work of the Red Cross Society.

He was made a Justice of the Peace for Bristol in 1902, received his Baronetcy in 1904 and by 1910 was Chairman of the Imperial Tramways Company and had been responsible for the existence of electric tramways in London, Dublin, Coventry and Middlesborough besides the system in his home city.

The Bristol Tramways Company was formed in 1874 and services commenced on 9 August 1875 on the tramway which it leased from Bristol Corporation. Horsebuses were introduced in 1877 and ten years later the title The Bristol Tramways and Carriage Company Limited was adopted to recognise its involvement in various forms of road transport including haulage, taxis and hearses. Electric trams first ran in Bristol in 1895 and by 1908, when the Tramway was extended from Horfield to Filton, the City had an expanding network of tracks and a large fleet of rolling stock. From the Filton terminus, motor 'buses connected with Thornbury and other outlying areas.

After initial but less than successful trials with Thorneycroft, Berliet and Fiat 'buses, B.T.&.C.C. started to build 'buses in two galvanised iron sheds in the village of Filton which also served as a depot for country services in South Gloucestershire. The bus works has often been referred to as the ''tram sheds'' but there is no evidence to suggest that trams were actually built at Filton. Bristol's trams were, up to 1920, all built by outside firms such as Milnes of Birkenhead, The Bristol Carriage & Wagon Company and twenty-one were imported from the American Car Company in the USA.

The flight on Friday 18 December 1903 at Kittyhawk, North Carolina of a heavier than air machine built by the brothers Orville and Wilbur Wright attracted little attention in this Country apart from a short passage in the Daily Mail. By 1909 the French pioneers including the Voisin Frères and Henri Farman had become the leaders in Europe. Emile Stern, who had contacts with The Tramways through his association with Charron cars, provided the French connection when Sir George White wanted to tap this expertise from across the English Channel.

At a B.T.&.C.C. shareholders' meeting on 16 February 1910 Sir George announced his intention to commence building flying machines for which he could foresee a lucrative market. Three days later on 19 February he formed The British & Colonial Aeroplane Company Limited with a capital of £25,000 and three other companies; The Bristol Aeroplane Company Limited, The Bristol Aviation Company Limited and The British & Colonial Aviation Company Limited each with a nominal capital of £100. The Registered Office of all four companies was 2 Claire Street, Bristol. The risk capital was subscribed by Sir George White, his son G. Stanley White and his brother Samuel White.

(Above)
SIR GEORGE WHITE, Bart., LLD., J.P.,
Founder and Chairman of the British and Colonial Aeroplane Co., Ltd., President of the Bristol and West of England Aero Club.
Portrait from ''Flight'' 7 December 1912.

The new trading company took over the sheds at Filton from The Tramways and Sir George issued instructions to young George Challenger in no uncertain terms for the removal of the 'buses so that aeroplanes could be built. The 'buses were hastily dispersed to any Tramways depot that had space available and this unsettled state of affairs continued until a new home for 'bus manufacture was found at Kensington Hill, Brislington in February 1912.

The name Bristol is now inseparable from the history of aviation although, ironically, the birthplace of the many thousands of aeroplanes bearing this name has never been a part of the City and County of Bristol. Originally in Gloucestershire, Filton was at least a mile from the northern limit of Bristol and is now in Avon County.

The close ties between the two related companies were evident throughout the lives of both enterprises and were very much due to personal contacts. Charles Challenger was General manager of the Tramways while his son George, who was a Foreman at the 'bus works, became involved in the building of the first Bristol aeroplanes. After Sir George White died on 22 November 1916, just when his newest empire was becoming firmly established, the family connections remained at all levels and people migrated from one Company to the other — some people coming to Filton from the Motor Constructional Works even as late as 1983.

The year AD1985 marks the seventy-fifth anniversary of aerospace manufacture in Bristol. From simple beginnings in two iron sheds, the Filton Works has grown steadily in the intervening years and now covers a 730 acre site employing 8,000 people. Products too have changed radically from wood and wire biplanes through supersonic monoplanes to the fringes of outer space. The following pages give just an insight of Filton activity from the first flight of a Bristol aeroplane on 30 July 1910 until the present day with a hint of what may transpire in the remainder of Bristol's first century in the air.

(Above)
FILTON HOUSE
Old Filton House pictured prior to 1910 when it was still a luxury residence. It was later acquired by the British and Colonial as offices. Many early Bristol aeroplanes were conceived within its walls.

(Below)
BRISTOL C40 (1908)
***AE771*, the first of many thousands of 'buses to carry the Bristol name, at work on the Victoria Rooms to Suspension Bridge service in the early years of this Century.**
Both the chain driven C40 chassis and the 16 seat saloon body were built in the two iron sheds at Filton which are now part of S03 machine shop.
From a postcard in the M.J. Tozer collection.

Early Types

Zodiac

To get production under way at Filton, a licence agreement was made with Société Zodiac, Paris to build the Zodiac 52B biplane which was based on a design by the Voisin brothers.

An airframe and engine were obtained from Paris and hurriedly assembled in the Filton bus sheds in 1910 for the Olympia Aero Show in March. One of the largest of thirty full size flying machines on view, the workmanship of the "Bristol Zodiac" attracted favourable attention. In design, it resembled the Voisin pusher biplane on which Henri Farman had made his early flights and had a wing span of 33ft-3in and a length of 39ft-3in.

When the show closed, the Zodiac was returned to Filton to be prepared for its first flight planned for April. Eventually after a number of modifications it was shipped by road in crates to Brooklands motor track on 10 May.

At Brooklands it was assembled by Sydney Smith assisted by Collyns Pizey, the assistant engineer, and Labouchère. On 28 May, piloted by M. Pierre Edmond, it made its first attempt at flight but was underpowered with the Darracq water cooled engine. Neither Sydney Smith nor his assistant Leslie MacDonald could coax it of the ground at all. Finally, on Edmond's advice, it was dismantled and returned to Filton.

Five other airframes had been started at Filton but when the first refused to fly the project was abandoned and the licence terminated. Instead, a new biplane was designed by George Challenger.

Challenger

The Bristol-Challenger Biplane, unofficially but now irrevocably known as the "Boxkite", was the first aeroplane to go into production at Filton.

After the abandonment of the Zodiac, a new biplane was devised by George Challenger along the lines of the French Henri Farman biplane and incorporating parts of the frame of the Zodiac. Two prototypes were built, (works nos.7 and 8), the first having a 50hp Gregoire engine and the second a 50hp ENV although these were later replaced by 50hp Gnomes. In July 1910, no.7 was taken by road to Larkhill on Salisbury Plain where it was reassembled and flown on 30th July by Edmond to a height of 150ft at the first attempt.

In its original form the Challenger Biplane had a wing span of 33ft, was 38ft-6in long and stood 11ft high: almost the same as the Zodiac. The composite frame used steel tubing joined by sockets and braced by piano wire rigging. Wooden ribs gave shape to the varnished fabric covering the wings, tailplane and control surfaces. With a loaded weight of a mere 900lb it could fly at all of 40mph.

Number 8 with ENV engine was sent to Scotland in company with no.7 for the Lanark Aviation Meeting on 8 August 1910. No.7 was flown successfully, again by Edmond, and both Biplanes returned south to act as training machines at the Bristol flying schools at Brooklands and Larkhill.

A month after the Lanark meeting the Challenger Biplane gained the distinction of making the first ever

(Below)
ZODIAC BIPLANE (1910)
The Zodiac biplane at the Olympia Aero Show in March 1910.
Numerically the first aeroplane to carry the Bristol name, the Zodiac was built in France and it was intended to follow it with another five machines built under licence at Filton.
When the Zodiac shown here refused to fly, the project was abandoned but some parts already made were incorporated into the first true Bristol aeroplane — the Challenger Biplane or 'Boxkite'.

(Above)
BRISTOL CHALLENGER BIPLANE (1910)
Biplane (Works no.7) bearing competition no 19 being flown by Edmond at Lanark in August 1910.
Number 7 was the first Filton designed and built aeroplane and the first Bristol machine to fly. It first flew on 30 July 1910; five months after the formation of the British & Colonial Aeroplane Company limited.

military flight during army manoeuvres on Salisbury Plain when no.9 was flown by Capt. Dickson.

Making and marketing aeroplanes was not alone sufficient to ensure the success of the Bristol venture and it was essential to give potential purchasers the opportunity to learn to fly. The Company had therefore decided to set up its own flying schools. Always practical yet at the same time concious of the power of publicity, Bristol flying schools were set up at Larkhill on Salisbury Plain and at Brooklands. Larkhill was a good site because it was not densely populated yet was close to Tidworth and Bulford Army camps where it would attract the curious attention of Army officers. Brooklands was the focus of the motor sport and a good place to find prospective flyers and customers.

After the success of no.7, the 50hp Gnome engine was adopted for production and no.9, the first Biplane to be built with this engine was sent to Larkhill School in September 1910. The next machine, no.10 together with no.11 as spare, was shipped to Australia on a Bristol mission where it was flown early in 1911 at Perth, Melbourne and Sydney.

Production was brisk and by the end of 1910 sixteen Biplanes had been completed including two of a new type (nos.12 and 15) which had extensions to the tips of the upper wings thereby increasing the span to 46ft-6in. These were sent on a Bristol mission to India where they were demonstrated to the Viceroy of India, the Governor of Bengal and the heads of the civil and

(Below)
BRISTOL CHALLENGER BIPLANE (1910)
Biplane no.12 with extended upper main plane at Maidan racecourse, Calcutta on 6 January 1911 during the Indian sales tour.
Number 12 was the first Biplane with the larger wing span and had a 50hp Gnome engine. After the tour it returned to the U.K. as a school machine at Larkhill.

military services at Maidan racecourse, Calcutta, on 6 January 1911. Several flights were made by M. Jullerot before a huge Indian crowd and, afterwards, the mission was invited to participate in cavalry manoeuvres in the Deccan. The Biplane gave a good performance despite the very hot weather and rough terrain.

A military version of the Extended Type followed which had a more powerful 70hp Gnome engine, larger fuel and oil tanks and three rudders (later reverting to two). The British Government eventually became interested in the Challenger Biplane but not before the first nine of the Military Type had been sold to Russia. Biplanes were sold to the newly formed Air Battalion and Royal Naval Air Service. Included in the 53 Military Biplanes, which became the general school biplane in production from January 1911 to October 1914, were two machines with 60hp Renault engines.

An Improved Military Biplane was exhibited at Olympia in March 1911 which had the wing span increased to 51ft and had a nacelle around the pilot to protect him from the slipstream and was in fact a rudimentary form of cockpit. Only three of this Improved type were eventually built.

A competition variant of the Challenger Biplane (no.44) was built for Maurice Tetard and the Circuit de l'Europe Race and was flown on 30 May 1911 but did not complete the course because of engine trouble. Another Biplane (no.69) was rebuilt by Gabriel Voisin using smaller wings and without the front booms. After testing at Larkhill it was rebuilt as a Standard Biplane.

Three other types of biplane were designed by

(Above)
BRISTOL CHALLENGER BIPLANE (1910)
Biplane no.16 with three rudders at Filton in 1910.
Number 16 was fitted with an ENV engine and extended wings in 1911 to make it an all British aeroplane to compete for the £500 Manville Prize which it won when flown by Howard Pixton.

(Below)
BRISTOL-CHALLENGER MILITARY BIPLANE (1911)
Biplane no.19 as built with 50hp Gnome engine and three rudders at Larkhill in 1911.
The military version of the Challenger-Biplane (Boxkite) had extended upper wings, larger fuel and oil tanks and 70hp Gnome engine. Early examples were test flown with 50hp Gnomes but re-engined before delivery. No. 19 was shipped to Russia but later returned to Filton where it was rebuilt as Biplane no.134.

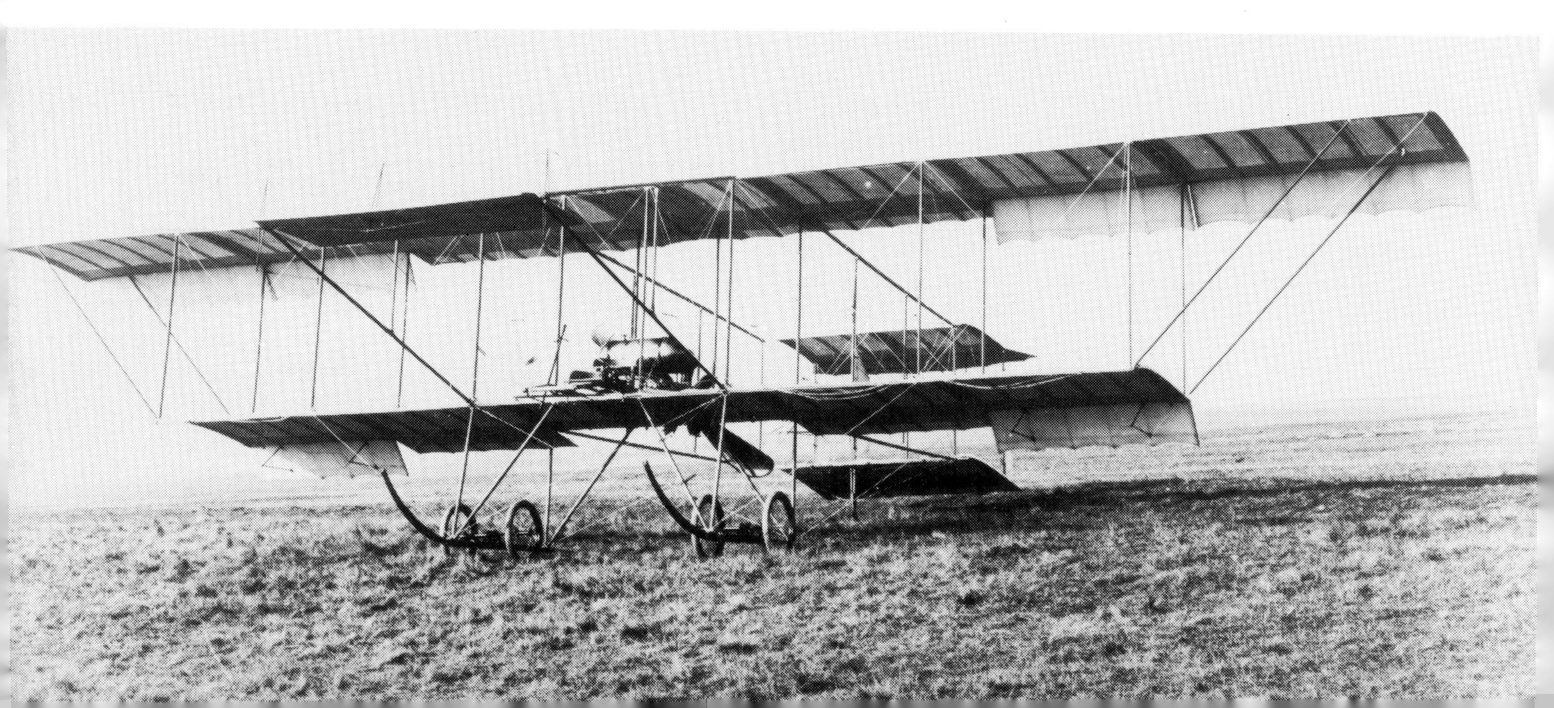

George Challenger which, although not the same as the original Challenger Biplane, were based on similar ideas.

A 2-seat biplane glider similar to the Challenger Biplane (boxkite) was built in 1910 to the private order of Sir George White for the Bristol and West of England Aero Club of which he was President. It was smaller than the Biplane and unpowered although it was designed so that an engine of about 30hp could be added later. First flown on 17 December 1910 at Keynsham it survived until about 1912 but was repaired several times in the intervening years.

A single seat racing biplane no.45 was designed by George Challenger and Capt. Dickson for Maurice Tabeteau to compete in the Circuit de l'Europe Race of 1911. Officially described as the Type-T Biplane (for Tabeteau?) it was also known as the Challenger-Dickson Biplane. It had a 70hp Gnome engine driving a pusher propeller positioned at the rear of a bath-like structure.

The front framing was stronger than the normal Biplane and incorporated upswept skid rails like a sleigh to prevent the machine nosing over when landing on rough ground. M.Tabeteau successfully completed the race of just over 1000 miles which encompassed a circuit from Paris to Brussells, then to Hendon near London and back to Paris. Less than a quarter of the 38 starters finished the race.

For the Circuit of Britain Air Race of 1911, four new machines (no's.51-54) designated Improved Type-T Racing Biplane were constructed, the first three having 70hp Gnome engines while no.54 had a 60hp Renault. The ''Daily Mail Racers'', unofficially dubbed after the sponsor of the event, had two vertical rudders at the extreme ends of the elevator instead of being closely spaced as in no.45. The race was something of a fiasco

(Below)
BRISTOL GLIDER (1910)
Bristol Glider at Filton when new in 1910.
The Bristol Glider was built for the Bristol and West of England Aero Club as a gift from Sir George White and was an unpowered derivative of the Challenger Biplane (Boxkite) then in production.
It first flew in December 1910 and survived until about 1912 despite the efforts of some pilots to write it off.

(Bottom)
BRISTOL TRACTOR BIPLANE No.33 (1911)
Biplane no.33 outside the former bus sheds at Filton — now a small part of S03 machine shop. The new Filton House now stands adjacent to the site occupied by the tree in the background.

as far as Bristol was concerned and the type was further discredited when no.51, which had been sold with a 50hp Gnome engine to a private buyer, crashed whilst being flown 'two up' thus killing the pilot.

One Type-T airframe was taken over by Eric Gordon-England for experiment. With a 60hp ENV engine driving a tractor propellor, the Challenger-England Biplane (works no.59) had the front booms removed completely and the original empennage replaced by a single fin and rudder within the existing framework. It first flew in November 1911 but crashed at Larkhill in May 1912 killing a spectator.

While the Challenger Biplane (boxkite) was establishing the production line at Filton, if the term 'production' is appropriate for the days when traditional coach building methods were being used, experiment was required to find a successor. George Challenger and Collyns Pizey were charged with the task and learned to fly at larkhill as an essential prerequisite to setting down to work. They were given practical assitance by Grandseigne and Versupay.

The Bristol Tractor Biplane no.33, also known as Grandseigne's Racer and Grandseigne's Tourer after its co-designer, was of very advanced design for its year of construction. It was an attempt to build an aeroplane with performance superior to that of the 'box-kite' creations favoured by the early pioneers.

Powered by a forward mounted 50hp Gnome engine it had a box section fuselage of steel tubing and wood braced by piano wire and covered by fabric. The wings built up on single spars were fabric covered on upper and lower surfaces to present a true aerofoil section. Only four struts were used between the two sets of wings to reduce drag as much as possible in an attempt to achieve air speeds previously considered possible only in a monoplane.

After the Olympia Show in March 1911 where no.33 was exhibited in company with Monoplane no.35 and the latest Improved Military Biplane no.31, it was taken by road to Larkhill for flying. It was, unfortunately, wrecked while attempting a maiden flight and was not repaired.

It had been intended to display a monoplane at Olympia in 1910 to complement the Zodiac but one was not available in time.

The first Bristol monoplanes were nos.35 and 36 built in 1911. Their design was the work of George Challenger with the scientific assistance of Archibald Low for which reason they were also called Challenger-Low Monoplanes. They had a triangular section fuselage along the lines of the Antoinette monoplanes and wings of Bleriot pattern were built up on single spars to allow wing warping. Before the advent of the aileron it was the practise to warp or twist the wings in opposite directions to make the aeroplane bank in a turn. A 50hp Gnome engine with tractor propeller was mounted at the front of the tubular steel fuselage. Wire bracing for the wings was anchored at a pylon above the cockpit and to the two wheeled, centre skid, undercarriage.

Number 35 was sent to Larkhill in February 1911 for testing but 'flight' was no more than a series of hops. In the following March it was shown at Olympia while its twin, no.36, was sent to St. Petersburg, Russia in April. The type cannot be considered a success but much was undoubtedly learned from it.

A similar machine, no.70, was built in France by Gabriel Voisin and bought by the Company for trial. It proved to be too heavy to fly and was abandoned along with the two Bristol Monoplanes.

(Below)
BRISTOL CHALLENGER-LOW MONOPLANE (1911)
Designed by George Challenger and Archibald Low, two of these tractor monoplanes (no's 35 & 36) were built in 1911.
Early attempts at flight with the first one was most likely only a series of hops rather than real flight and some damage was sustained.
Number 35 was shown at Olympia in March 1911 while no.36 was taken to Russia for exhibition in April. Further development was abandoned in favour of a new range of monoplanes designed by Pierre Prier.

(Top)
BRISTOL TYPE-T BIPLANE (1911)
Improved Type-T biplane no.52 with 70hp Gnome engine.
The original Type-T biplane, no.45, was built for Maurice Tabuteau and was followed by four of an Improved Type-T biplane (no's 51-54). A further more powerful variant no.78 was not completed.

(Centre)
BRISTOL CHALLENGER-ENGLAND BIPLANE (1911)
Originally a Challenger 'Type-T' biplane, no.59 was rebuilt by Eric Gordon-England in 1911.
It had a 60hp. ENV engine driving a tractor propeller and was flown at Larkhill on Salisbury Plain where it is pictured here in December 1911. After a landing mishap six months later, it was dismantled.

(Lower)
VOISIN MONOPLANE (1911)
Number 70 was a single seater monoplane of tubular steel construction designed by Gabriel Voisin and built in France. Very little is known about it apart from this rare photograph taken at Larkhill on Salisbury Plain in 1911.

Bristol Prier Monoplanes

Pierre Prier joined the British & Colonial Aeroplane Company Limited in June 1911 as an instructor at the Company's flying schools at Larkhill and Brooklands. He had become famous in April 1911 when, as chief instructor at the Bleriot flying school at Hendon, he made the first non-stop flight from London to Paris. Prier was a qualified engineer with great technical ability in addition to being a skilfull pilot thus making him a valuable asset to Bristol.

Prier's first design for Bristol was a single seater monoplane powered by a 50hp Gnome engine and known as the Bristol-Prier P1. Three machines (works numbers 45, 46 and 57) were built in 1911 for entry in the Gordon Bennett Aviation Cup and Circuit of Britain Race competitions of that year but were unsuccessful.

Number 57 was converted into a single seat school machine with an Anzani engine, followed later by number 46. Larkhill school received no.56 in June 1911 while no.57 was sent to Brooklands on 3 February 1912.

A two seater version was constructed concurrently with the solo machines and the second of these, no.71, was given a show finish for exhibition at the Paris Salon to which it was delivered on 10 December 1911. To prove that the Bristol was as good as it looked, Valentine flew a similar machine, no.74, around the Eiffel Tower before the opening of the show. Sales were made to the Italian Army, and to Spain as well as to the War Office bringing the total production to ten of this type.

An improvement to the Prier two-seater was made by Captain Bertram Dickson who, in conjunction with Prier, extended the fuselage by thirty inches and modified the tail-plane. Orders for the Prier-Dickson 2-seat monoplane were received from Spain, Germany, Italy and the Royal Flying Corps as well as two similar machines with 70hp Gnome engines sold to Turkey. The Prier-Dickson became very popular with repeat orders coming from Germany as late as 1913.

Three side by side 2-seat Prier Coanda school monoplanes were built under the guidance of Henri Coanda after Prier had left the Company. A total of 34 machines of the various Prier types was built.

(Above)
BRISTOL PRIER P.1 MONOPLANE (1911)
Pierre Prier's first design after his arrival at Filton was the P.1. single seater monoplane powered by a 50hp. Gnome engine for racing competitions.
Number 56 shown here was the second of the three that were built and was "pranged" by Prier himself but was repaired and flown again.
In November 1911 it was fitted with an Isaacson engine to make it an all-British aeroplane for competition with other British 'planes flown by British pilots.

(Right Upper)
BRISTOL PRIER SCHOOL MONOPLANE (1911)
Seven of these single seater advanced trainers were built and, in addition, P.1. no's 46 and 57 were converted to this form.
They had 35hp. Anzani radial engines and most were used at Larkhill School. However, no.81 was sold to Spain in March 1912 and no's 95 & 96 went to Italy in May of that year. Number 98, pictured, was delivered to Larkhill in September 1912.

(Right Centre)
BRISTOL PRIER 2 SEAT MONOPLANE (1911)
Number 72, one of the "short fuselage" two seaters at Larkhill in 1912.
Eleven of this primary trainer version of the Prier. P.1 were built and most were sold to the War Office but no.83 was exported to Italy and no's.76, 84 and 90 eventually went to Spain.

(Right Lower)
BRISTOL PRIER-DICKSON MONOPLANE (1911)
Number 82, the first of the Prier-Dicksons at Larkhill in 1912 before it went to Spain to replace no. 83 which had crashed there.
Nine Prier-Dicksons were built with 70hp Gnome engines plus no.155 which was a rebuild of the wrecked no.130. Most of these "long fuselage" 2-seaters were exported with no.82 going to Spain, no's.86 and 88 to Turkey, no.89 to Italy and 85 & 155 to the German Army.

THE
BRISTOL

THE BRITISH
THE BRISTOL
AND COLONIAL
THE BRISTOL

THE
BRISTOL

Bristol Gordon England Biplanes

E.C. Gordon-England came to Bristol in the autumn of 1911 as a pilot but before the year was out he had become involved in the rebuilding of the Type-T Biplane no.59.

He proceeded to design another tractor biplane G.E.1 (no.64) which had a square section fuselage with two seats side by side and with stout square tipped wings of 33ft-8in span. The G.E.1 army cooperation biplane first flew on 12 May 1912. A 4-cylinder in-line 50hp Clerget engine drove the propeller via a chain concealed behind the radiator and after the fitting of a balanced rudder it was a sturdy, easy to fly machine but was underpowered. It was sold to Deutsche Bristol-Werke on 19 June 1912 but returned to Filton later that year and was subsequently scrapped.

The G.E.2 with round tipped wings of 40ft span was larger than the G.E.1 and two examples were built, no.103 with a direct drive 100hp Gnome engine and no.104 with a 70hp Mercedes Benz driving the propeller by chain reduction. Both were similar to no.64 but had a gap between the fuselage and the lower wings to afford greater clearance between the propeller tips and the ground. Both were sent to Larkhill for a military competiton but were unsuccessful due mainly to engine problems.

An enquiry from Turkey resulted in Gordon England's third design, G.E.3, of similar size to G.E.2 but with a circular section fuselage housing tandem cockpits, long range fuel tanks and a 80hp Gnome engine. Two machines, nos.112 and 113 were built but early flights of the first one showed up a structural weakness of the wings. Struts were added between the fuselage and the upper wings but the type was not totally satisfactory and they were never delivered. The fuselage of the second G.E.3 is believed to have been incorporated in the Coanda hydroplane no.120.

(Left Upper)
BRISTOL GORDON-ENGLAND GE1 BIPLANE (1912)
GE1, in as built condition, outside the bus sheds at Filton (now S03 machine shop). Note the rope tying the undercarriage to the flagpole to stop it flying away during engine runs.
The GE1 was a side-by-side 2-seater army co-operation biplane driven by a 50hp. Clerget water cooled engine and first flew on 12 May 1912.

(Left Lower)
BRISTOL GORDON-ENGLAND GE2 BIPLANE (1912)
Bearing its competition number 12, the first GE2 with Gnome engine was posed at Larkhill in August 1912.
The GE2 was larger than the GE1 and had a 100hp. Gnome air cooled engine in the first machine and a 70hp. water cooled Daimler in the second.

Bristol Burney Hydroped Biplanes

In October 1911 Lieut. C.D. Burney R.N., who had been impressed by the work of the Italians Forlanini and Guidoni with hydrofoils, pursuaded the Bristol Directors to apply the principle to aircraft. Lt. Burney's intention was to employ hydrofoils and water propellers to propel an aircraft to such a speed and height that it could alight from the water more easily than an aeroplane with floats.

At first it was proposed to modify the G.E.1 but as this was earmarked for Germany a new machine was sanctioned. The Admiralty considered that the work should be kept secret so an experimental department or ''X-dept'' was set up. Lt. Burney's ideas were translated into fact by Frank Barnwell and Clifford Tinson, both of whom had only recently joined the Company.

For preliminary trials the Burney X1 (no.92) was taken to Dale near Milford Haven on 9 May 1912. It had the hydrofoils and water propellors on the lower ends of legs or 'hydropeds' that replaced the usual undercarriage. It was found that the 80hp Canton-Unne engine did not have sufficient power for the air and water propellors at the same time and was unable to accelerate the aeroplane to take off speed.

When testing resumed in September it had been redesignated X2 due to the many changes made to it, particularly the hydropeds and water propellers, during the summer. It was still under powered but was towed as a glider behind a Naval craft. During these experiments it rose clear of the water but stalled, was wrecked and was abandoned in favour of a larger craft.

The Burney X3 (no.159) which superseded the X2 was to be fitted with a 200hp Canton-Unne engine but for initial testing a 80hp Gnome was used and slats were fitted in place of the wings. During later trials with the wings attached it was damaged when it hit a submerged sand bank and the project was abandoned as impractical.

(Above)
BRISTOL GORDON-ENGLAND G.E.3 BIPLANE (1912)
This official portrait of the G.E.3 Biplane was taken at Filton in November 1912 after extra bracing had been added to restrain the top wings.

(Below)
BRISTOL BURNEY X2 (1912)
Burney X2 Hydroped Biplane in 'flight' while being towed behind a fast naval craft off the Pembrokeshire coast in September 1912 and shortly before it crashed.

(Above)
BRISTOL-BURNEY X3 (1913)
Burney X3 off Pembrokeshire during taxiing trials using water propellers in 1913 with slats in place of the wings and with a 80hp. Gnome engine.

Bristol Coanda Monoplanes

Henri Coanda succeeded Pierre Prier and was appointed technical advisor to the British & Colonial early in 1912. Son of General Coanda, the Roumanian War Minister and Commander-in-Chief, Henri was a talented engineer who had acquired a sound technical education in France. He had studied under Eiffel and had used his wind tunnel in Paris to test some models having advanced features before coming to Bristol.

His first design at Filton was a school monoplane, no.77, having tandem cockpits furnished with basket seats and windows in the sides. It used a 50hp Gnome engine in a circular cowl of Grandseigne design and was delivered to Larkhill on 27 March 1912 where it was flown experimentally for several months.

A side by side two seat school machine with dual controls was also made at about the same time and the first of these, no.80, was in use as a trainer at the Bristol schools until 1914.

Five similar monoplanes followed on from no.77 with no.132 going to Italy and four others to Roumania Export orders were also forthcoming from these countries for the side by side two seater, Italy receiving two and Roumania three, while the last one, no.177, became a trainer at Larkhill.

For the 1912 military competition held in June and July 1912, Bristol submitted two Coanda monoplanes, nos.105 and 106 with 70hp Renault engines, as well as the two G.E.2 biplanes. After early mishaps, Harry Busteed and Howard Pixton flying the monplanes shared third place with a British Deperdussin for which feat they won £500 each. The Company profited too in getting an order for the two aircraft after the event.

The Coanda Military Monoplane, improved by increasing the wing span from 40ft to 42ft-9in and by reducing the structure weight, became very popular. Two were ordered by Italy and another for the personal use of Prince Cantacuzene of Roumania, while Pixton demonstrated a fourth at the Roumanian Army manoeuvres in Bucharest. Number 131 was given a show finish and exhibited, in company with a Coanda School Monoplane, at the Paris Salon in October 1912. Both were bought by Italy. Roumania, faced with a war with Bulgaria, also ordered ten of the Military type.

A succession of crashes of monoplanes of various makes brought a ban on monoplane flying by Royal Flying Corps pilots although this did not extend to the Royal Naval Air Service. Investigation continued into 1913 and was eventually lifted but the delay lost sales of monoplanes.

Coanda's least successful monoplane was no.111, an enlarged Military Monoplane with a 70hp engine, nicknamed the 'Elephant'. It was delivered to Larkhill with two sets of wings of different shape but never flew properly with either set.

Coanda had great confidence in his monoplanes and demonstrated the strength of the wings by turning one over on its back outside the shops and loading it with sandbags. However, with the continued uncertainty to some degree, it was wise and practical to consider biplanes as well.

(Right Upper)
BRISTOL-COANDA SCHOOL MONOPLANE (1913)
Coanda monoplane no 132 at Filton in 1913 before being sold to the Italian Government as the tenth Bristol machine to go to that country.
Powered by a 50hp Gnome engine, six of these trainers were built in 1912/13 and five were exported to Italy and Roumania. (Henri Coanda's native country).

(Above)

BRISTOL-COANDA COMPETITION MONOPLANE (1912)

Coanda monoplane no.105 with modified rudder which gained third prize when flown by Harry Busteed in the 1912 military competition.

The competition monoplanes no's 105 and 106 were 2 seat military machines with 80hp Gnome engines.

(Below)

BRISTOL-COANDA MILITARY MONOPLANE (1912)

Works number 118 the first production machine ready for the road.

After the success of no 105 in the 1912 competition twenty further Coanda military monoplanes were built but due to War Office disfavour towards monoplanes most were sold overseas or eventually converted to biplanes.

BLERIOT
SOCIETE ANONYME DES MOTEURS SA
Bristol
MONOPLANES
NAG

Bristol Coanda Biplanes

On 14 February 1913, His Majesty King George V opened the fourth International Air Show at Olympia. Bristol exhibited two machines — a two seat monoplane and a new biplane with a 70hp Renault engine known at Filton as the BR7. The biplane represented Coanda's latest ideas for a weight lifting military biplane and incorporated many standard details currently in use on monoplanes.

The Admiralty placed an order for two biplanes of similar pattern — one a land plane with an 80hp Gnome engine and the other a seaplane having a single, central float and two stabilising wing tip floats.

In its first trial flights the BR7 proved too heavily loaded with the monoplane derived wings and a new set was put in hand. These gave better results but the Renault engine was never entirely satisfactory and only seven BR7's were built: no mean achievement nevertheless.

The Coanda Hydroplane no.120 purchased by the Admiralty was a private venture and was sent from Filton to Cowes in March. It was a fairly large biplane with a wide central float designed by Oscar Gnosspelius. The mahogany float became waterlogged rendering the aircraft too heavy to fly so a plywood float was substituted but burst during a forced landing and the the machine was lost.

In 1913 the Coanda Monoplane no.121 was rebuilt as a biplane to become the prototype TB8 biplane. The TB8 was Coanda's most successful design with no less than 53 being built new, or rebuilt from Coanda Monoplanes. Various Gnome, LeRhone and Monosaupape-Gnome engines were used ranging from 50 to 110hp.

After the loss of the Coanda Hydroplane no.120 the TB8 prototype no.121 was fitted with a pair of floats made from the Gnosspelius float and was christened TB8H while retaining the same constructors number. It was later rebuilt again and given sequence number 205.

The TB8H was not the only unique Coanda biplane for there were several other 'one-offs'. Before the First

(Left Upper)

Coanda Monoplane (seq.no. 153) and Coanda BR7 biplane (seq.no. 157) on show at Olympia in February 1913.

(Left Centre)

Model of proposed Coanda monoplane with unusual propulsion which was tested in Gustav Eiffel's wind tunnel in Paris circa 1913.

(Left Lower)

BRISTOL-COANDA CENTRAL FLOAT SEAPLANE (1913)

Coanda Hydroplane no.120 at Cowes, Isle of Wight before trials in March 1913.

It was unfortunately lost when it crashed into sea on 15 April 1913 after engine failure. It was a 2 seater with a 80hp Gnome engine.

(Below)

BRISTOL-COANDA BR7 (1913)

The first Coanda BR7 (SN157) in flight at Larkhill in 1913 with H.Pixton at the controls.

Official prejudice against monoplanes led to Henri Coanda's first biplane design at Filton which used a 70hp Renault engine. Seven of these 2 seat machines were built with the hope of exporting them to Spain but this did not happen. Six were sent to Larkhill and used as school machines while the seventh was retained at Works for development. The title BR7 was derived from Biplane Renault 70hp.

World War Olympia was the shop window for new Bristol aeroplanes and at the 1914 Show the Coanda GB75 was unveiled. Differing from the TB8, yet owing something to its predecessor, the GB75 (no.223) with 75hp Mono-Gnome engine was intended for Roumania.

Built in response to a request from the French Government, the Single Seat Armoured biplane (S.S.A. no.219) had a 80hp Clerget engine, bullet proof cockpit and was flown at Larkhill in May 1914. During subsequent flying it was damaged but was delivered to France in the summer of 1914.

When war broke out in August 1914, all civil flying was banned and all available aircraft and engines were requisitioned for military use. As a result a new Coanda design, PB8. no.199, a pusher biplane with 80hp Gnome engine, never got into the air. The GB75 was re-engined with a 80hp Gnome and delivered, with two TB8's, to Farnborough. Three other TB8 biplanes were taken over by the RNAS for patrols of the southern and eastern coastline to give warning of the approach of enemy ships, aeroplanes and Zeppelin airships. The War Office order for twelve TB8's was delivered from 26 September and a final order of these, for trainers with the RNAS, was completed in early 1916.

Filton then settled down to building Government designed and financed B.E. biplanes which had started in 1912 with the B.E.2. Henri Coanda himself returned to his native Roumania.

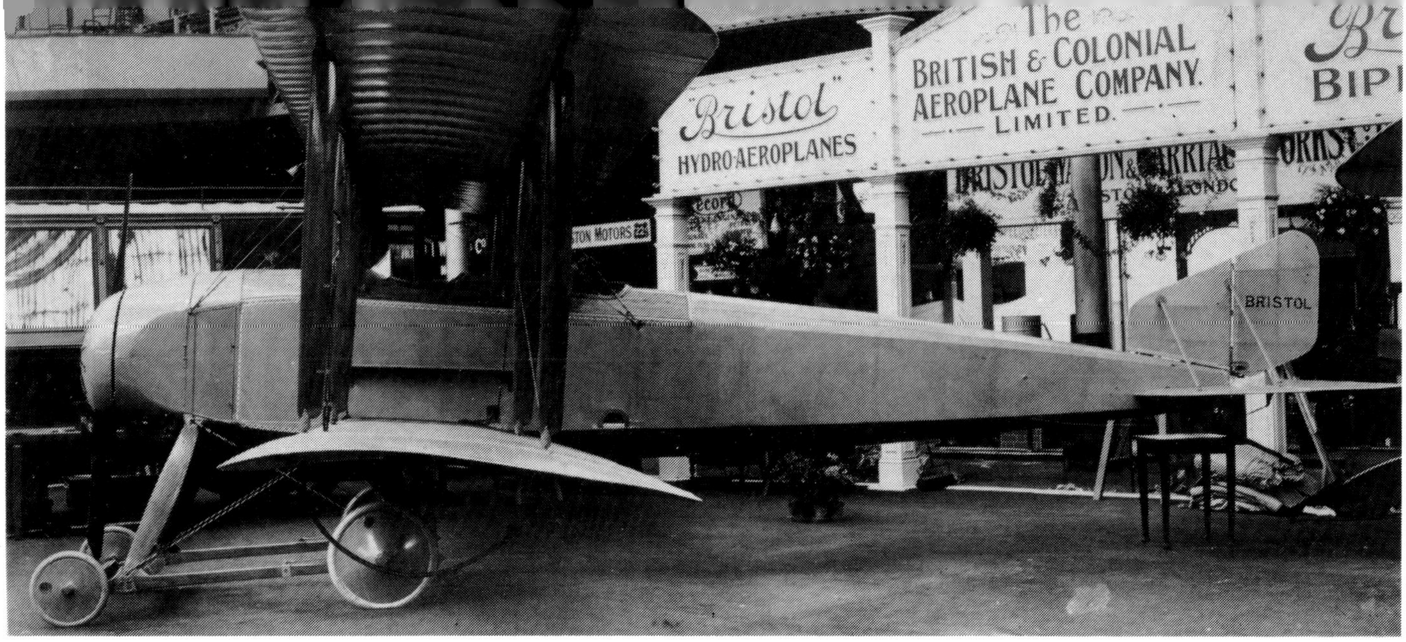

(Left Upper)
BRISTOL-COANDA TB.8 (1913)
Howard Pixton and M. Henri Jullerot with the first TB.8 biplane at Larkhill in July 1913.
Originally a Coanda monoplane, no.121 was rebuilt as the prototoype TB.8 biplane with 80hp Gnome engine. (Tractor Biplane 80hp Gnome)

(Left Lower)
BRISTOL-COANDA TB8H HYDROPLANE (1913)
Coanda TB8H Hydroplane at Dale, Pembrokeshire in September 1913.
After the loss of the Coanda Hydroplane no.120 the TB8 prototype no.121 was fitted with floats and became TB8H.

(Above)
BRISTOL-COANDA GB75 (1914)
GB75 on display at Olympia, London in 1914.
One machine, no.223, was built for Roumania with a 75hp Mono-Gnome engine but due to the War was diverted to the Royal Flying Corps with 80hp Clerget. It first flew in April 1914.

(Below)
RAF BE.2D/E
Bristol did not only build Bristol ideas and during the Great War hundreds of aircraft were built to Royal Aircraft Factory designs. This is a BE.2D fitted with BE.2E wings.
From the experience gained in building these rather frail machines and from the reports from RFC pilots who flew them Bristol went on to design the rugged and successful Scout and Fighter biplanes.

World War One

Rapid expansion of the Filton Works resulted from the start of the Great War on 4 August 1914. The iron sheds, which had been extended almost as soon as 'The Tramways' had been ousted by the new British & Colonial in 1910, became the Erecting Hall for the early types. However, a new brick-built Erecting Hall was constructed at the western end of the sheds and had an adjoining fitting shop. Additional brick detail shops were put up on the south wall of the sheds filling up the corner bounded by the terraced houses on Southmead Road and that well known hostelry, The Anchor. The flying ground facing the houses in Fairlawn Avenue was also built over to provide mess rooms (now medical dept.), a womens' centre to cater for the expanding female work force, a woodmill and plating shop.

Finished aircraft were taken in sections out of the main gate in Homestead Road near Filton House and down the hill (A38) to a new level flying ground near Gypsy Patch Lane. Six new hangars were later built there by German prisoners of war.

By 1914, Frank Barnwell had already begun to assert himself as a designer in his own right. He had been involved with the design of the Burney boats and the Coanda machines but would have been subject to the authority of the senior men.

Before leaving the Company, Coanda had in fact started work on another single seat monoplane SB5 no.183 but work was stopped, with the fuselage still unfinished, when it was realised that the design weight would be exceeded. Barnwell was given authority to develop it and produced a single seat biplane, no.206, of 22ft span and 19ft-9in long with a 80hp Gnome engine. It was taken to Larkhill near Stonehenge in February 1914 and flown by Harry Busteed. In March it was exhibited at Olympia with the GB75 tractor biplane and because it was smaller than the latter it was given the epithet Baby Tractor Biplane. At Easter it was rebuilt with larger wings and circular engine cowling for the 1914 racing season.

Two further prototypes, nos. 229 and 230, were built from scratch and named Scout B — the Baby Tractor being renamed Scout A in retrospect. Of the 161 early production examples called Scout C (built at Brislington), 74 went to the Royal Naval Air Service. These fast, unarmed, reconnaissance machines gained a favourable reputation with Royal Flying Corps pilots in France. The definitive form of the Scout was produced in four versions — Scout D Gnome, Scout D LeRhone, Scout D 100 Mono and Scout D 110 Clerget.

Government policy in 1913 and early 1914 was to centralise aeroplane design at the Royal Aircraft Factory at Farnborough. Production of these official designs was then passed over to the various privately owned aircraft makers and from the end of October 1914 the whole of the Filton Works was devoted to the B.E.2C biplane. As a result, the technical staff at Filton was relegated to the less demanding and more boring routine drawing office work dealing with RAF drawings. The experimental 'X' dept., was closed and the prospects for innovation seriously curtailed.

Not having a challenging future, Barnwell left Bristol to enlist in the RFC and was followed by many of the drawing office staff who joined one or other of the three British armed forces.

After the superiority of the German aircraft over the Royal Aircraft Factory biplanes had become obvious there was a revitalisation of the private sector. Barnwell, now Captain Barnwell, returned to Filton in

(Below)

BRISTOL BABY TRACTOR BIPLANE (1914)

Lord Carberry starting from Hendon in the London-Paris-London Air Race in 1914.

The original Baby Tractor airframe was sold to Lord Carberry who installed a 80hp LeRhone engine for racing. He flew it in several events but it was lost when he ran out of fuel on the way back from Paris and had to ditch it in the English Channel.

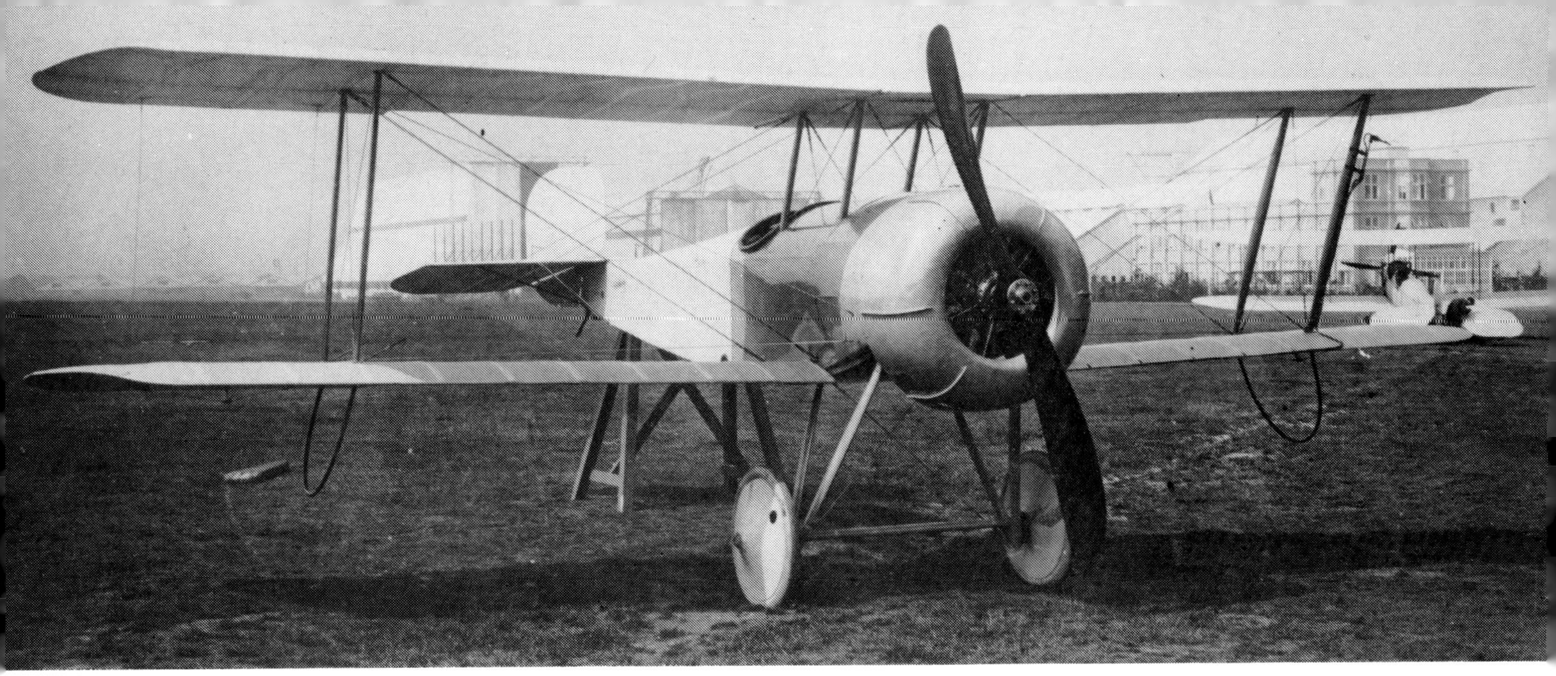

(Above)
BRISTOL SCOUT B (1914)
First of the two Scout B biplanes with 80hp. Gnome engine at Farnborough in September 1914.

Two further prototypes of the Scout were built and were similar to the Baby Tractor (Scout A) as modified with circular engine cowling.

At the outbreak of War, both Scout B's were sent to France where the favourable reports from the RFC pilots resulted in production orders which were delivered as Scout C.

(Below)
BRISTOL SCOUT C (1915)
Scout C, seq.no.1255, during trials on board HMA *Vindex,* a former Isle of Man steamer converted with a flying off deck, on 3 November 1915. It was used for attacks on Zeppelin airships as they crossed the Channel to bomb London.

the summer of 1915 and set up a new design office with L.G. Frise, an honours graduate from Bristol University, as his assistant. The Scout was in full production at the Motor Constructional Works of 'The Tramways' using labour trained at Filton. Having had front line experience, Barnwell turned his attention towards a combat biplane.

The first of Barnwell's designs on his return to Filton in 1915 was a biplane originally drawn in September as the Twin Tractor with two *RAF4a* engines but later revised as the Twin Tractor A with two Beardmore engines. It first flew in May 1916 but only two prototypes, registered *7750* and *7751* were built. A similar fighter, F3A, with a 250hp Rolls Royce engine was proposed but not built.

To meet a need for a 2-seat fighter, Barnwell created the S2A which had a wide fuselage seating the crew side by side but otherwise copied the Scout D 110 Clerget. Two prototypes, sequence no's 1377 and

(Right)
BRISTOL SCOUT D 100 MONO (1916)
***8980* with Mono Gnome engine in RNAS service.**
A third batch of Scout D biplanes was produced in 1916 for the RNAS and were identified *8951* to *9000*. All fifty machines had 100hp Mono Gnome engines which made them faster, albeit a little heavier, than the earlier Scouts.

(Below)
BRISTOL T.T.A. (1916)
Twin-Tractor fighter biplane at Filton in 1916.
Originally intended to use *RAF4a* engines, two prototype Twin Tractor fighters were built for the War Office using a pair of 120hp Beardmore engines.
The first machine flew in May 1916 indicating a speed of 87mph. The pilot sat in the rear cockpit with the gunner in the nose to give a wide range of fire from the two front mounted Lewis guns.

1378, were constructed in May and June 1916. They were not perpetuated and spent their lives as school machines at Filton and the Central Flying School, Upavon.

Aircraft with increased speed were demanded by RFC pilots to reduce the losses of machines and men in the aerial battles over Europe. After trials with a modified Scout D, Barnwell devised a high wing monoplane using a 110hp Clerget engine with a domed spinner. Flight trials of the single seat M1.A no.1374 in September 1916 achieved a speed of 132mph — about 30mph faster than a Scout D. Four more monoplanes were ordered which, with a modified fuselage to take a 100hp LeRhone engine and a Vickers gun, became M1.B. The production version, M1.C. of which 125 were built, was considered after trials to be unsuitable for the Western Front. They were eventually sent to the Middle East to equip no.47 sqdn. RFC at Salonika and 77 sqdn. at Dasra to replace Scouts.

In pursuit of his ideal for the perfect combat biplane, Capt. Barnwell designed a series of biplanes in 1916. The first, a 2-seat biplane R2A, with a 120hp Beardmore engine was succeeded by the R2B having a more powerful 150hp Hispano-Suiza. Neither was built but the work evolved into the F2A, the first of the Bristol Fighters. Two prototypes were erected, the first (RFC serial *A3303*) with a 190hp Rolls Royce engine was first flown on 9 September 1916 followed by Hispano Suiza engined *A3304* on 25 October.

The expected performance of both prototypes was exceeded in official trials and a production order for fifty F2A's was placed. A subsequent order for 200 more was changed to cover a revised form, F2B, the 'real' Bristol Fighter.

Production was speedily undertaken by Bristol Tramways at Brislington in order to equip RFC squadrons, including nos.11 and 48, in readiness for the 1917 spring offensive. With the ending of production of the official B.E. biplanes, a Fighter assembly line was also established at Filton. When the War Office

(Above)
BRISTOL S2A (1916)
The first S2A, RFC serial *7836,* when new at Filton in 1916. Derived from the Scout D, the S2A or Scout 2 Aside was a 2-seat trainer with 110hp Clerget engine and two were built.

decided to re-equip RFC squadrons with Bristol Fighters large orders were received but these far outstripped the possible capability of Filton and Brislington. Consequently, the manufacture of Bristol Fighters was subcontracted to the motor industry and other large workshops.

From the 250th Fighter the 275hp Rolls Royce *Falcon III* engine was standardised but shorages created a variety of F2B's having other engines. Some of the alternatives such as the Sunbeam *Arab* were not fully developed and teething troubles hampered delivery schedules. The Fighter was chosen for manufacture in the USA but of the 4000 ordered only 27 had been accepted at the Armistice.

Up to 11 November 1918 when the War ended, 1349 Fighters had been delivered from Filton and 853 from Brislington. Production continued until June 1919 by which time 2081 had been built at Filton, 1045 at Brislington and 1621 by outside contractors. This was not the end of the F2B, however, but more of this anon.

As the Great War progressed there was the risk of a severe shortage of prime timber for airframe construction and Bristol was contracted to build two prototypes of an all-metal version of the Bristol Fighter for testing. Named MR.1 it was a 2-seat biplane and the fuselage was a double skinned aluminium monocoque structure. Wings made of wood were fitted to the first prototype which had a 140hp Hispano-Suiza engine and was flown in October 1917 while the second one powered by a Wolsley *Viper* engine had steel wings made in Gloucester. Both machines, seq. 2067 and 2068, were built by Bristol Tramways and Carriage Company at Brislington because Filton was at full capacity with F2B production.

Contemporary with the MR.1, the single seat tractor biplane Scout E was intended to make use of a new 10-cylinder radial engine, the 200hp *Cruciform.* An alternative 'pusher' version was also proposed but neither biplane got off the drawing board because the *Cruciform* engine was discontinued.

The Scout F which followed and was similar to these stillborn schemes was arranged to suit another new engine, the 200hp Sunbeam *Arab.* Six Scout F prototypes were ordered with the *Arab* water cooled V8 engine but, due to the poor reliability of the engine, only two were completed and flown in 1918.

The third Scout F airframe was adapted to take yet another new engine, the Cosmos *Mercury* designed by L.F.G. Butler of Brazil, Straker & Co., at Fishponds, Bristol. It was successful in trials but not put into production because the War ended and the *Mercury* engine was cancelled. Of the three remaining airframes that were started, one was completed but not engined and the other two were abandoned.

Efforts to design a successor to the Bristol Fighter F2B led to three schemes for a Bristol Fighter C using 200hp Salmson, 300hp A.B.C. *Dragonfly* and Bentley *BR2* engines respectively. These schemes were not built but culminated in the Badger biplane.

Built around the *Dragonfly* engine, the Badger was a 2-seat fighting biplane with two fixed forward firing guns and a Scarff ring mounted gun to cover the rear. Three were ordered and construction began in the summer of 1918. On its maiden flight in February 1919 the first Badger, *F3495,* crash landed but was rebuilt with another *Dragonfly* installation having a more pointed cowl. The next one, *F3496*, was fitted with a Cosmos *Jupiter* engine when first built in 1919 for comparison with *F3495.* Both machines were sold to the Air Board after *F3496* had had a *Dragonfly* engine installed and with service equipment and armament added.

The Badger or Bristol Fighter C came too late to see active service and the third prototype was cancelled because the first had suffered from instability in flight. Barnwell used the redundant parts together with a new slab-sided fuselage, 230hp *Puma* engine and as the Badger X, it first flew on 13 May 1920 but was 'pranged' by Barnwell soon afterwards. The Badger X was a laboratory machine to compare the results of wind tunnel testing with full scale flying.

A further order was eventually placed for a biplane with a 500hp Cosmos *Jupiter* engine — Badger II. Registered *J6492,* it was sold to the Air Council in the spring of 1920 but was used by the Company as a test bed for the *Jupiter* engine which had become a Bristol product on the acquisition of Cosmos Engineering on 29 January 1920.

The closing years of Bristol's first decade as a major aeroplane producer were marked by the introduction of two contrasting types — the gigantic Braemar triplanes and the diminutive Babe biplane.

G-EAVO
G

2
Bristol

(Left Upper)
BRISTOL MI.A. (1916)

Prototype M1 monoplane scout as built in 1916.
Built as a private venture, the M1.A monoplane was devised to replace unsuitable Royal Aircraft Factory machines on the Western Front.

The unarmed prototype M1.A was built with a 110hp Clerget engine and was sold to the Air Board for evaluation. It was later modified to M1.B standard and became a school machine.

(Left Centre)
BRISTOL M1.C (1916)

G-EAVO was one of the M1.C monoplanes rebuilt for civilian use in 1920 and is seen here at Filton.

The production version of the M1 monoplane was designated M1.C. It had a 110hp LeRhone engine and was armed with a single Vickers gun mounted on top of the engine firing through the propellor.

125 machines were built as fast armed scouts and equipped Middle East squadrons. After the War the Company bought back 3 of them for conversion to sporting machines for resale. One of these *G-EAVO* was later sold to a Spaniard and became *M-AFAA.* Another machine was sold in the USA while a third was kept at Filton.

(Left Lower)
BRISTOL 'M.1.D.' LUCIFER MONOPLANE (1922)

The 'M.1.D.' Monoplane started life in 1916 as an 'M.1.B.' with Clerget engine and had subsequently been bought back by the Company after the War, rebuilt and given the civil registration *G-EAVP,* with the intention of reselling it as a sporting 'plane.

In 1922 it was converted to a flying test bed cum racing machine to develop the new Bristol 'Lucifer' 100hp, 3-cylinder radial engine.

Painted scarlet and black with white lettering, it won the Aerial Derby Handicap at Croydon in that year. It was entered for other events but crashed whilst racing in 1923.

(Below)
BRISTOL F2A (1916)

First prototype F2A (RFC serial *A3303*) at Filton in 1916 in as built condition with vertical side radiators.

A3303 and the second prototype A3304 were built at Filton but fifty production F2A fighters were built by The Bristol Tramways & Carriage Co.Ltd., at Brislington.

(Bottom)
BRISTOL FIGHTER F2B (1918)

Demonstration of starting a Bristol Fighter using a Hucks starter mounted on a car.

(Above)
Bristol Fighters including *F4712* being built in the Erecting Hall at Filton in 1918.

(Below)
BRISTOL FIGHTER F2B PUMA (1918)
F2B *H6058* with 240hp Siddeley *Puma* engine built by the Austin Motor Company at Longbridge, Birmingham in 1918.
Due to a shortage of Rolls Royce *Falcons* other makes of engines were tried with varying degrees of success. Several hundred *Puma* engined Fighters were built before orders were suspended at the Armistice.

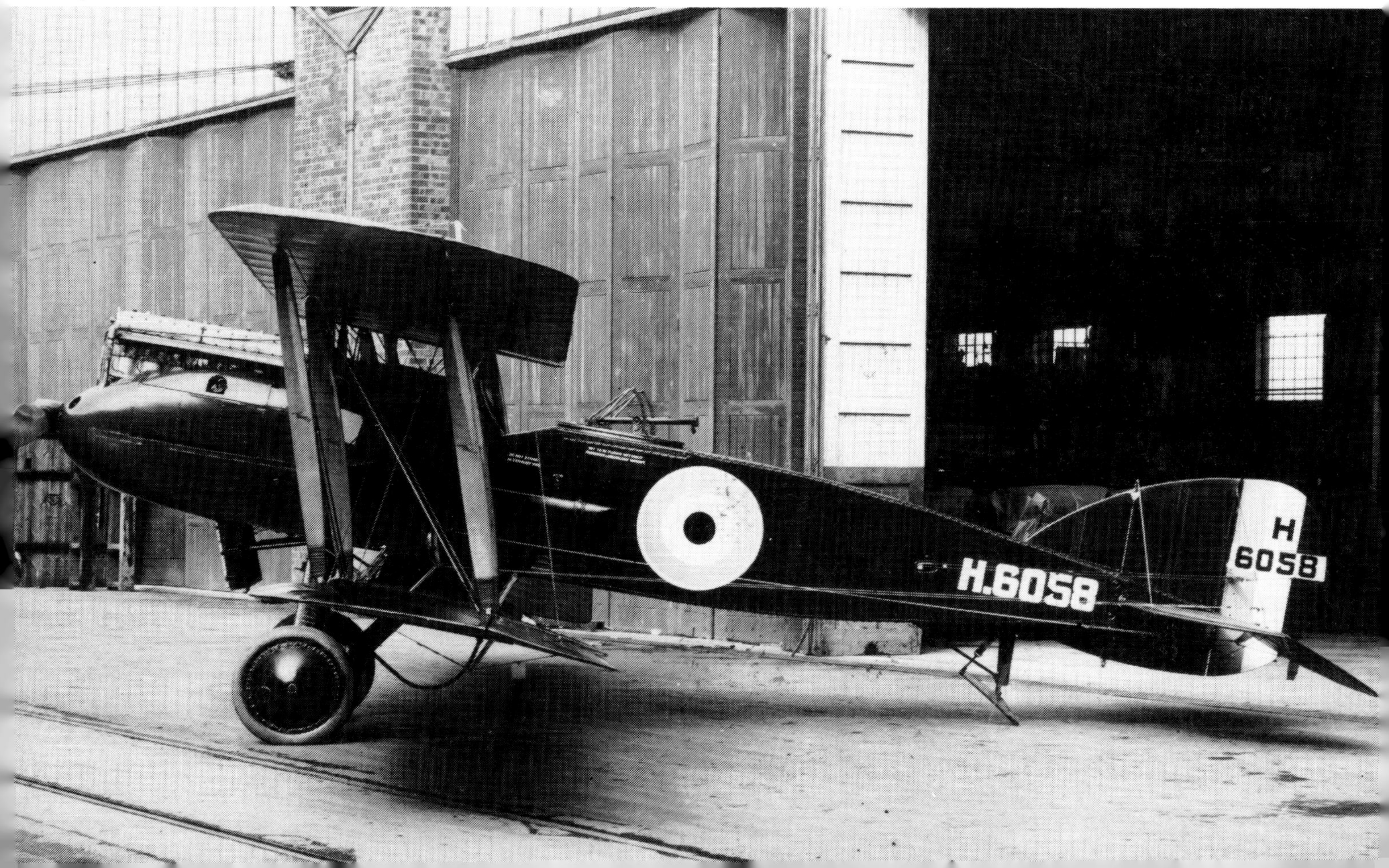

(Above)
Bristol Fighter *C4630* (seq.no.1980) captured by the Germans in 1918.

(Right)
BRISTOL FIGHTER F2B (1918)
***F2B* no*C801* of 5 squadron RAF Risaplur in 1926. It was built at Filton in 1918 (Works no.3201).**

(Below)
Bristol Fighter *B1124* interned in Holland in 1918.

(Above)
BRISTOL FIGHTER USA-01 (1918)
American built F2B with *Liberty 12* engine at Buffalo, New York in 1918.

When the USA entered the Great War a licence agreement was arranged for the manufacture of large quantities of Bristol Fighters as victory seemed a long way off.

The first Curtiss F2B's with the 400hp *Liberty* V12 engine were not a success but later versions built in Ohio with the smaller *Liberty 8* were an improvement.

(Below)
BRISTOL FIGHTER F2B ARAB (1918)
Arab engined F2B at Filton in 1918 with the original oval casing.

Attempts to substitute the Sunbeam *Arab* engine in place of the R.R. *Falcon* proved unsuccessful due to rough running and poor reliability of the *Arab*.

Over 1000 aircraft built either at Filton or by contractors were intended to have *Arabs* but the actual total is uncertain. Many airframes were put into store through lack of engines and did not enter service during the 1914/18 war.

(Right Upper)
BRISTOL M.R.1. METAL BIPLANE (1918)
Studio photograph of *A5177,* the first M.R.1. of 1918, superimposed onto a Filton background.

(Right Centre)
BRISTOL SCOUT F. (1918)
Arab engined first prototype Scout F at Filton in January 1918.

(Right Lower)
BRISTOL SCOUT F.1. (1918)
The third Scout F prototype with Cosmos *Mercury* engine at Filton in 1918.

A-5177

(Left Upper)
BRISTOL F2C BADGER I (1919)
F3495, **the first of the Badger I's, as built with A.B.C. *Dragonfly* engine at Filton in 1919.**

(Left Centre)
BRISTOL F2C BADGER I (1919)
The second Badger I, *F3496,* with Cosmos *Jupiter* air cooled engine at Filton in 1919.

(Left Lower)
BRISTOL BADGER X (1920)
Puma engined Badger X under construction in the Experimental Flight Shed at Patchway (now West Works).

(Right Upper)
BRISTOL BADGER X (1920)
Badger X, or 'Barnwell's Weekender' with 230hp Siddeley *Puma* engine at Filton in 1919.
It was the first Bristol Aeroplane to be entered in the Civil Register and received the number *K110* — later changed to *G-EABU.*

(Right)
BRISTOL BADGER II (1920)
J6492 **as built with Cosmos Jupiter engine in 1920.**

(Below)
BRISTOL 'BADGER II' (1920)
'Badger II', *J6492,* with Bristol *Jupiter II* 9-cyclinder radial engine and experimental cowling in 1921.
The last of the four 'Badgers' was designated 'Badger II' and was used as a flying test bed for the new *Jupiter* engine.

Braemar

Originating in November 1917, as a long range bomber for attacking German industrial targets, and Berlin itself, in reprisal for raids on London by *Gotha* bombers, the triplane was of advanced design. It was intended to carry 250lb bombs stowed internally and to have a range of at least 1000miles. A central engine room was proposed with each pair of engines driving via shafting a four bladed tractor propellor on the centre wing at each side of the aircraft.

As Barnwell was fully occupied with the Badger he delegated the detail design to W.T. Reid. A simpler form was devised by Wilfred Reid using four Siddeley *Puma* engines mounted back to back in tandem pairs on the centre wing and an order was obtained for three prototypes.

The size of the Braemar presented severe difficulties and they were built under the direction of Arthur Suddes in the Experimental Flight Shed (now adjacent to the A38 overpass at Gipsy Patch Lane). When completed they were 'launched' sideways out of the hangar doors on bogies running on rails set into the floor.

Braemar mk.1 with four 240hp *Puma* engines was completed in the summer of 1918 and flown by F.P. Raynham — achieving 106mph. The second prototype, Braemar mk.II had 400hp *Liberty* engines but did not fly until 18 February 1919 — three months after the Armistice. Both Braemars had a wing span of 81ft-8in, were 52ft-6in long and 20ft high but the Braemar II was about 20mph faster than the first one and had a better rate of climb despite the increased gross weight.

With the ending of the War, the third Braemar was cancelled but the components already made were incorporated with a new cabin fuselage into a 14 passenger airliner designed by Reid. After its first flight in May 1920 when it reached 135mph, the Pullman was exhibited at Olympia in the summer of 1920 causing something of a sensation due to its size. It was then delivered to Martlesham Heath for testing by the Air Ministry and showed great promise but did not go into passenger service and was finally dismantled.

Several schemes for triplanes were prepared by Reid after the War but remained as 'paper aeroplanes'. One scheme was, however, adopted and two prototypes of a triplane freighter, the Bristol Tramp were built. Barnwell's idea of a central engine room was revived and four Siddeley Puma engines mounted in the fuselage drove a pair of 4-bladed propellers via clutches, gearing and shafts — the idea being to eliminate the drag caused by wing mounted engines.

The drive was troublesome with the result that neither Tramp was flown but they were later used at Farnborough as ground rigs for the testing of the engines and transmission until abandoned. The Tramp was the largest of the Braemar family having a wing span of 96 feet.

(Below)
BRISTOL BRAEMAR I HEAVY BOMBER (1918)
The first Braemar triplane C4296 at Filton in 1918 at the time of its first flight.
Built for bombing raids on German targets, the Braemar I had four Siddeley *Puma* engines arranged in tandem pairs and carried a crew of four including two gunners. It was used at Farnborough for flight testing until its demise circa 1920.

(Right Upper)
BRISTOL BRAEMAR II HEAVY BOMBER (1919)
***C4297,* the second Braemar prototype for the RAF, had more powerful *Liberty* engines and other improvements. It first flew in February 1919 and was flown at Martlesham Heath until about 1921 when it was wrecked in a duel with a hanger.**

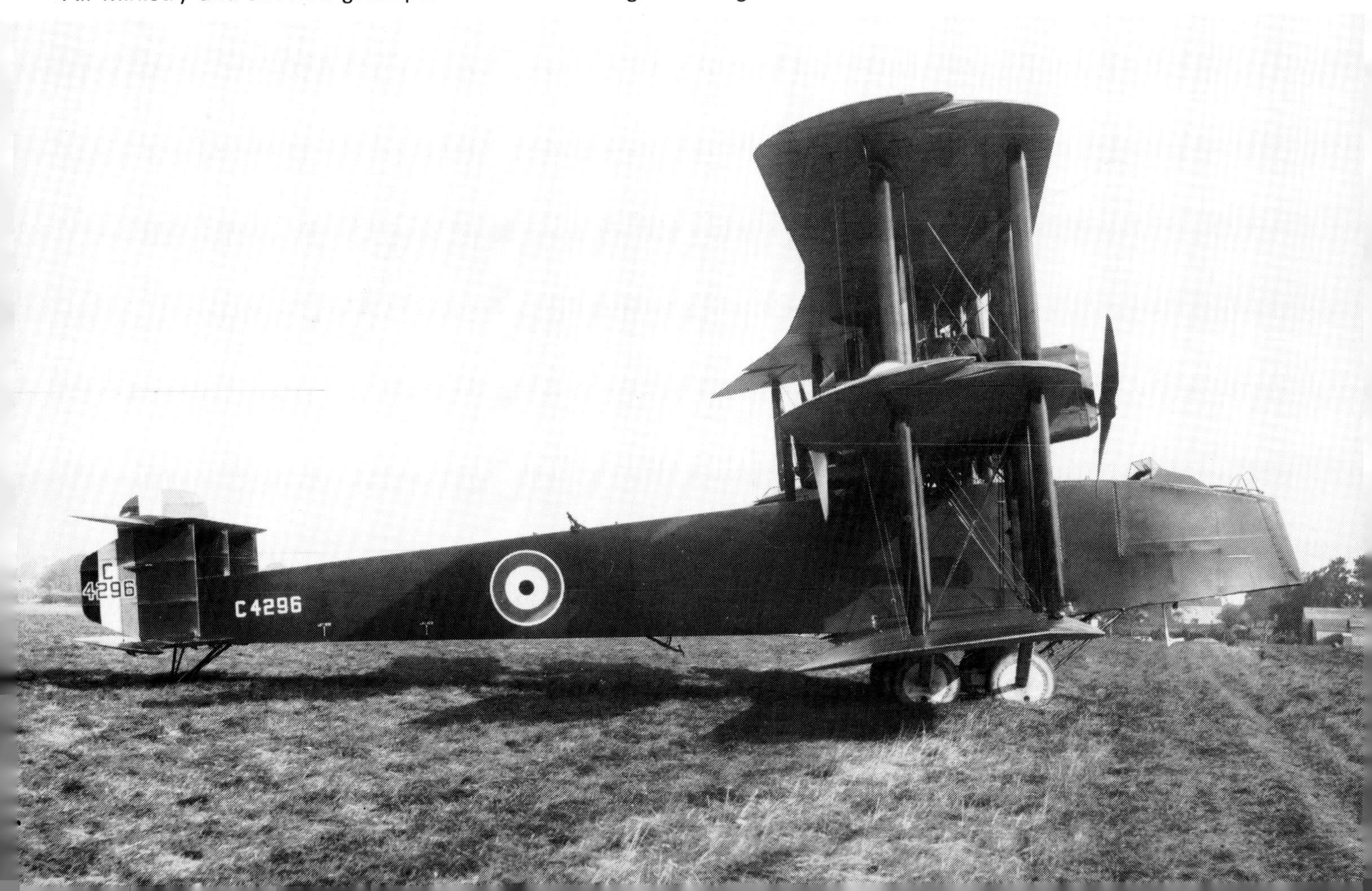

(Below)

BRISTOL 'PULLMAN' 14-PASSENGER TRIPLANE. (1920)

Pullman triplane and Babe biplane posed together at Filton in 1920.

The third Braemar prototype was built with a larger cabin fuselage as a 14 seater passenger transport with the revised name of Pullman.

C4298 first flew in May 1920 and was exhibited at Olympia that summer after which it was sold to the Air Board for further flight testing at Martlesham Heath.

Two tractor and two pusher propellers were driven by four American *Liberty* engines mounted back-to-back on the centre wing giving a maximum speed of 130mph.

(Left)
INTERIOR OF BRISTOL 'PULLMAN' (1920)
The passenger accommodation of the 'Pullman' was received favourably by the critics of the time but it is fortunate for present day jet setters that comfort has improved since then.

(Below)
BRISTOL TRAMP TRIPLANE (1922)
***J6912*, the first of the Tramps, at Filton early in 1922 prior to ground running.**
Two of these development aircraft were built to test a new method of propulsion which had first been proposed by Frank Barnwell in 1917 for a bomber and later as a 40 passenger Pullman. Neither Tramp ever flew.

Babe
Bristol's smallest aeroplane with a mere 19ft-8in span, the single seat Babe was a contemporary of the gigantic Bristol triplanes. Intended to be a purely sporting machine, the Babe was designed to use the 60hp A.B.C. *Gadfly* engine but this did not materialise. Capt Barnwell substituted a 35hp *Viale* engine, which was his own personal property, so that the Babe could be flown by Cyril Uwins on 29 November 1919.

Before any production could be contemplated a reliable engine was essential and the 40hp Siddeley *Ounce* seemed to have good prospects. A second Babe was built with an *Ounce* in time for display at the first post-war Paris Salon de l'Aeronautique in December 1919.

The unreliability of the *Ounce* in later testing prompted another search for a suitable power plant and two development LeRhone engines were obtained from France. The *Viale*-engined Babe mk.I and a third airframe were rebuilt to take the LeRhone to become Babe mk.III — both machines being flown between December 1919 and April 1920. One of the Babe III's was later rebuilt with experimental monoplane wings but never flew in this form. When an engine reliable enough to satisfy the demands of civil flying, by perhaps inexperienced pilots, could not be found the Babe project was allowed to lapse.

(Right Upper)
BRISTOL BABE mk.1 (1919)
Babe mk.1 as first flown with *Viale* engine by C.F. Uwins on 28 November 1919.

(Right Centre)
BRISTOL BABE mk.III (1919)
Babe mk.III with LeRhone engine pretending to be swung in the wrong direction!
The Babe mk.1 with *Viale* engine and the another airframe were rebuilt in 1919 with 45hp. LeRhone engines and redesignated Babe mk. III.

(Right Lower)
BRISTOL BABE (1919)
The three Bristol Babes together in the hanger at Patchway in the 1920's. (Now part of Rolls Royce.)
Left: Babe mk II with Siddeley *Ounce* engine and right: Babe mk.III as rebuilt as a monoplane. Neither of these prototypes was ever flown.
The LeRhone engined Babe mk.III biplane in the background was a rebuild of the *Viale* engined Babe mk.I.

CHANGING FACE OF FILTON -2

The Works in 1921 after the rapid expansion which took place during the 1914-18 War. Golf Course Lane crosses in the foreground.

Bristol Aeroplane

Early in 1920 The British & Colonial Aeroplane Company Limited went into voluntary liquidation for the purpose of reconstruction. The Bristol Aeroplane Company Limited, which had also been formed in 1910, had its nominal capital of £100 raised to £1,000,000 on 9 February 1920 to become the trading company.

Unfortunately for this narrative, the type of product of the Company does not form a natural break to coincide with the change of constitution. Some aeroplanes that had been started in 1918 or 1919 did not come to fruition until the early years of the 'twenties. Conversely, other machines had their roots in the British & Colonial era: being adaptations of military types to civilian use.

The cancellation of all outstanding Wartime contracts in September 1919 had left the Company in a predicament of having large premises, a massive skilled workforce but slim prospects of making an adequate profit to offset this burden and to enable it to invest in the future.

At this juncture the Bristol Tramways once again came to the rescue but in an opposite manner to that received previously. B.T.&C.C. had built large numbers of aircraft when the safety of the Country was threatened and was in any case prohibited from carrying on its normal business. Six years without any 'bus construction had left the Bristol fleet severely depleted and it was opportune that the 'bus revival should coincide with the low ebb at Filton.

Bristol chassis having Bristol Aeroplane single deck 'bus bodies were exhibited at the Motor Shows of 1920, 1921 and 1923. The 1920 Show chassis still survives appropriately registered BAE592 but has been rebuilt with a lorry body by Amey Roadstone. Van and tanker superstructures were also built on Bristol chassis at Filton and work was obtained from Siddeley Motors in the shape of luxury car bodies. This non-aircraft work helped the Filton Works weather the opening years of the Roaring Twenties.

The large quantity of surplus Bristol Fighters available from the Disposals Board after the war influenced several attempts by the Company to market civil versions of the F2B. In 1919, a production Bristol Fighter, *H1460,* with a 275hp *Falcon* engine was converted to an unarmed light transport. A wicker chair and small

(Below)
BRISTOL AIRBUS (1921)
Siddeley cars and Bristol 'buses in the Erecting Hall (now MPS) in 1920. To make up for the shortage of aircraft orders, commercial work was obtained from sister firm Bristol Tramways at Brislington to build bodies for Bristol 4-ton and 2-ton chassis. Besides 'buses and vans, lorries, tankers and cars were bodied in the opening years of the 'twenties.

(Above)
BRISTOL COUPE (1919)
***H1460* the first of the Coupe and Tourer conversions.**

desk were provided in the rear cockpit which was enclosed by a triangular door and a hinged lid having celluloid windows. Three similar new F2B's were also rebuilt as 2-seat open courier transports in that year and had larger fuel tanks and dual controls.

Rolls Royce *Falcon* engines were not readily available except for RAF use but a plentiful supply of Siddeley *Puma* engines existed. With an eye on export sales ten *Puma*-engined Coupes seating two passengers in the enclosed rear cockpit were put on the market. The first was sold in the USA and it was hoped that others would follow but most of the Puma Coupes were eventually sold to Australian customers.

Between 1919 and 1921 twelve open 2-seat Puma Tourers (PT2S) and eight of a 3-seat version (PT3S) were sold. A Puma Seaplane Tourer was proposed for overseas markets but only one was actually built. Tourers left the Filton shops spasmodically until 1926 and included some with Wolseley *Viper* engines for Bulgaria.

Little work was involved in the Tourer conversions and the Works was saved from imminent closure in 1920 by a well-timed order for 215 Bristol Fighters mk.II. The F2B. mk.II, or "J-type", became the standard army cooperation biplane and in addition to the new machines hundreds of early F2B's passed through the Works for conversion. During 1922 the reconditioning of Fighters to J-type provided almost the entire aircraft workload at Filton.

In defference to the shortage of production work the Development Department was busy building experimental types. Some were purely racing machines to attract favourable publicity but others were a serious effort to meet official needs or to create a line of civil aircraft.

Not strictly a new design, the Seely Puma was a special machine for an Air Ministry civil transport competition in August 1920 in which it gained second

(Below)
BRISTOL F2B COURIER (1919)
***H1688*, second of the three dual control conversions of the Bristol Fighter.**

"Bristol"

(Left Upper)
BRISTOL PUMA COUPE 3 (1919)
First of the Puma Coupe 3-seat tourers, SN5891 at Filton before being shipped to the USA.
A batch of 10 tourers having Siddeley *Puma* engine were similar to *H1460* but seated 2 passengers in the rear cabin.

(Left Centre)
BRISTOL PUMA TOURER 3 (1919)
***M-AEAA* at Filton prior to delivery to Spain with its registration letters painted the side bulges.**
Eight 'PT3S' open tourers were rebuilt from *Puma* engined Fighters by widening the rear cockpit to seat two people side by side. One was sold to Instone's, 4 went to the United States and 3 to Spain.

(Left Lower)
BRISTOL PUMA SEAPLANE TOURER (1920)
The sole Seaplane Tourer on tow off Avonmouth in October 1920.
To attract foreign sales a seaplane version of the Tourer was devised and it was proposed to build two machines from existing Tourers but in fact only one, SN5873, was completed.

place. The Seely Puma was an enlarged and strengthened form of the F2B Tourer with a 240hp *Puma* water cooled engine. It was used for development flying after the trials and was rebuilt with a Bristol *Jupiter* engine in 1923.

Designed in 1919 and first flown in the summer of 1920 the Bullet was a development machine which could also be used in racing to publicise the virtues of the new *Jupiter* engine. It did not achieve the expected performance and was rebuilt with new wings of shorter span for the 1921 season. However, it was unsuccessful in that year but it managed second place in the 1922 Aerial Derby.

One of the last of Capt. Barnwells designs before his sojourn to Australia in the autumn of 1921 was a fighting monoplane termed MFA which could be converted into a 2-seat biplane named MFB. Two prototypes of the monoplane, serials *J6901* and *J6902,* and a biplane *J6903* were erected for use by the Air Ministry for flight evaluation of the *Jupiter* engine as well as the airframe. The convertible concept was probably a means of overcoming the official prejudice against monoplanes which still existed at that time but the type was not a success.

(Above)
BRISTOL PUMA SCHOOL TYPE B (1923)
***G-EBFS* when new at Filton.**
Based on the Puma Tourer (PT2S), the P.T.1923 Type B as the Puma School was also known, was yet another conversion of the Bristol Fighter.
Four were built from F2B's plus *G-EAXA* which was a further rebuild of Puma Tourer SN6120.

(Below)
BRISTOL VIPER TOURER (1923)
***G-BECA,* first of the Viper Tourers for Bulgaria in as-built condition with Hispano-Suiza type radiators.**
Two 2-seater Tourers with 180hp Wolseley *Viper* engine were built for the Bulgarian Government. They were also known as the Bulgarian Postal Machines.

(Above)
BRISTOL PUMA FIGHTER (1925)
One of six *Puma* engined advanced trainers sold to Greece.

Greece was not inhibited by the Treaty of Versailles from purchasing more powerful machines and received six *Puma*-powered advanced trainers which could be converted if necessary to fighters.

As delivered they did not have a gun mountings or gun gear fitted but the first three had Marconi wireless apparatus.

The same *Puma* engine supplied by the Greek Government was fitted in turn to all six machines for flight testing. The aircraft were then shipped without engine.

(Below)
BRISTOL VIPER TOURER (1926)
G-BEKA at Filton before shipment to Bulgaria in 1926.
A second batch of three *Viper* engined Tourers, also known as the Improved Bulgarian Tourer, were exported in 1926. They had oleo undercarriages, a larger tail fin with horn balanced rudder and different radiators. The 180hp Wolseley *Viper* engine was used because, as an ex-enemy country, Bulgaria was restricted to engines below 200hp.

(Top)
BRISTOL SEELY PUMA (1920)
Seely Puma *G-EAUE* as first built with Siddeley *Puma* engine at Filton in mid-1920.

(Centre)
BRISTOL SEELY SUPERCHARGER (1923)
Two seater Seely tourer with supercharged *Jupiter* engine at Filton in 1923.

In 1923, the Seely was rebuilt to test the Bristol *Jupiter III* radial engine fitted with an exhaust driven supercharger. After use as a flying test bed by the Company it was sold to the Air Ministry with the registration *J7004* and spent its days at Farnborough.

(Below)
BRISTOL BULLET (1920)
The Bullet after being rebuilt with smaller wings in 1921 being prepared for the Aerial Derby.

(Above)
BRISTOL MFB BULLFINCH (1923)
The third Bullfinch prototype, *J6903,* in the form of a two seater biplane.

By inserting a 3ft. long parallel section of fuselage incorporating a rear gunners position and second pair of wings into the MFA monoplane fuselage the MFB biplane was created.

Performance, load capacity and endurance were reduced due to the additional weight and these were the main reasons why the MFB was not ordered in quantity.

(Top)
BRISTOL MFA BULLFINCH (1922)
The first MFA single seat fighting monoplane with *Jupiter* engine in 1922.

(Right)
BRISTOL JUPITER RACER (1922)
Racer *G-EBDR* painted scarlet with white lettering at Filton in 1922 after wing bracing wires had been added but still retaining the large ailerons.

The Jupiter Racer was designed by W.T. Reid specifically to demonstrate the new Bristol *Jupiter* 9-cylinder radial engine in high speed flight. A bulbous fuselage was dictated by the need to completely bury the engine for minimum air resistance. After several memorable and near disastrous flights in 1922 it was abandoned primarily because its poor aerodynamic qualities did not give the pilot much hope of survival in the event of complete engine failure in flight.

The Ten Seater was the first new aircraft to be both designed and built at Filton after the Firm was reformed as the Bristol Aeroplane Company in July 1920 although the idea had been considered earlier. It used a 450hp Napier *Lion* water cooled engine and was first flown in June 1921 after which it received the civil registration *G-EAWY.* After trials by the Air Ministry to whom it had been sold late that year, it was put into service with Instone Air Lines, passing to Handley Page Transport Limited in February 1922.

Its successor, the *Jupiter* engined Ten Seater, known as the J10S, could seat eight passengers in addition to the pilot and wireless operator. As *G-EBEV* it flew in July 1922 and, after various demonstrations, was sold in 1924 to the newly formed Imperial Airways which had absorbed Instone. On the formation of Imperial Airways, a policy of using only multi-engined aircraft was adopted with the result that the J10S was no longer suitable.

G-EBEV was therefore flown to Filton and converted to a freighter capable of carrying almost ten tons of goods and returned to service with Imperial on the London to Cologne route. Entering service as a freighter on 22 July 1924 it had clocked up 150 flying hours by 23 August without major incident. It survived until about 1926 and was useful in proving the *Jupiter* engine in commercial operation.

Two other J10S airframes were constructed but not flown; one being sold with *G-EBEV* as spares and the other was revised as an air ambulance — the Brandon.

The partially completed Jupiter Ten Seater revised as the Brandon air ambulance was sold to the Air Ministry. With accommodation for two stretchers and four sitting cases, the Brandon was the first aeroplane to be built especially for that role. It made its first flight in the hands of C.F. Uwins on 19 March 1924 eventually being delivered as *J6997* to the RAF for service trials. The engine mounting was extended in 1925 to overcome a tendency to overheat and this also improved its flying stability. In peacetime there was little need for flying ambulances so the Brandon was not perpetuated.

While Barnwell was 'down under', Wilfred Reid moved up a rung to assume the title of Chief Designer. Reid had been responsible for most of the Ten Seater (Lion), J10S and Racer and went on to design a family of biplanes using the more docile 3-cylinder *Lucifer* — another Cosmos engine adopted by Bristol.

The Taxiplane, also known as the Lucifer 3 Seater or L3S was an open tourer seating two passengers side by side in the rear cockpit. *G-EBEW* first flew on 13 February 1923 and two others, *G-EBEY* and *G-EBFY,* followed but the type was too heavy for the *Lucifer.* A Certificate of Airworthiness could not be obtained and all three were later converted to L2S.

Concurrently with the building of the Taxiplane, six two-seat school machines with narrower fuselages were erected as primary trainers for the flying school at Filton. Originally known as L2S for Lucifer 2 Seater they were later called Lucifer School Machines, then Lucifer Trainers and finally Primary Training Machines or PTM for short.

Eighteen L2S were exported in 1926 including one for Bulgaria, five for Hungary and the remainder for Chile.

To flight test the new Bristol *Titan* engine a strengthened version of the Lucifer School Machine was specially built. It appeared with various *Titan* installations and was used in competitions but was scrapped at the end of the testing programme.

To demonstrate the *Jupiter* engine at minimum cost a Bristol Fighter was rebuilt with stronger front fuselage and landing gear to take the *Jupiter* radial engine. Three were actually converted but the type was considered unsuitable for further development as a fighter.

Contemporary with the Jupiter Fighter, the Jupiter School Machine was very successful as an advanced trainer to familiarise pilots with the new *Jupiter* engine. All seven of these had doped fabric covered airframes while the fuselages of the following fourteen were plywood covered for extra durability.

After the aborted attempt in 1919 to sell the Badger as a replacement for the F2B, a second attempt at an F2C was made in 1922. One prototype was constructed and called F2C but was later renamed Bloodhound. After its first flights it was rebuilt with modified wings and empennage in which form it was perpetuated by three further prototypes sold to the Air Ministry. It did not receive a production order but fighter orders were always hard to obtain in peacetime.

(Above)
BRISTOL TEN SEATER (LION) (1921)
G-EAWY, the first of the Ten Seater biplanes in its later condition with two-wheeled undercarriage at Filton in 1921.

(Left)
BRISTOL TEN SEATER (LION). (1921)
Interior view of *G-EAWY,* the first Ten Seater with Napier Lion engine as built in 1921.
Nine passengers were accommodated on three forward-facing single seats on either side of the aisle and a rearward-facing three person bench seat.

(Below)
BRISTOL JUPITER TEN SEATER (1922)
G-EBEV, the second ten seater (J10S) when new at Filton in 1922.
As it did not comply with Imperial Airways multi-engine policy it was returned to Filton in that year for conversion to a freight carrier.

(Above)
BRISTOL JUPITER EXPRESS FREIGHTER (1924)
G-EBEV **at Filton after being converted to a freighter for Imperial Airways.**

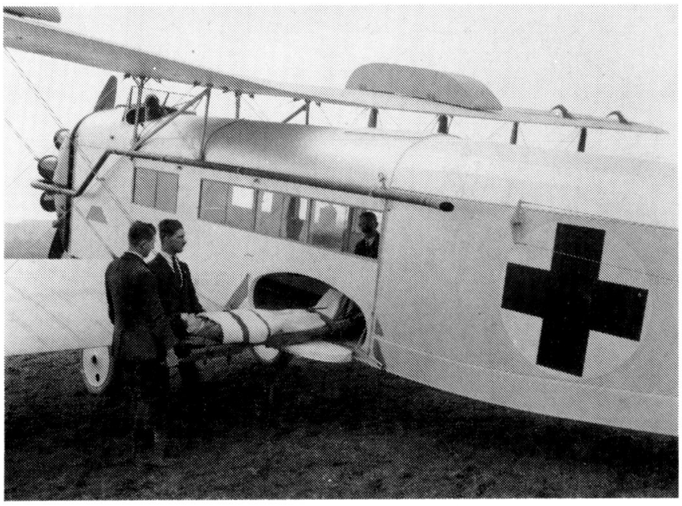

(Right)
BRISTOL BRANDON AT WORK.
A 'Patient' is being loaded through the stretcher door into the cabin of the Brandon air ambulance. *J6997* is shown in as built condition in 1924 with the short engine mounting.

(Below)
BRISTOL BRANDON (1924)
Bristol Brandon air ambulance at Filton in 1925 after being rebuilt with longer engine mounting.

(Above)
BRISTOL TAXIPLANE (1922)
Prototype Taxiplane *G-EBEW* as originally built as a three seater at Filton in 1922. Also known as the Lucifer 3 Seater or L3S the Taxiplane was a 3 seat open tourer using the Cosmos/Bristol 3-cyclinder *Lucifer* radial engine.

(Below)
BRISTOL LUCIFER SCHOOL MACHINE (1923)
G-EBFZ the prototype Lucifer School Machine in as-built condition. All six L2S trainers had a small fin and elevator but after the second batch of 18 in 1926 they were progressively rebuilt with larger tail surfaces.

(Right Upper)
BRISTOL LUCIFER SCHOOL MACHINE (1926)
G-BEPK at Filton in 1926 prior to being shipped to Bulgaria. The tail and fin was larger on this batch of eighteen.

(Right Centre)
BRISTOL LUCIFER SCHOOL MACHINE (1928)
The second Lucifer School Machine in racing trim seen at Filton in 1928.

G-EBGA was returned to the Works and 'cleaned up' for competition work. Fairings were fitted to the fuselage top, bottom and sides while aluminium closing pieces were fitted to the cockpit openings. New, larger, fuel and oil tanks were installed, a new cowling ring and pointed spinner added. It was the longest surviving machine and was sold to a private buyer in 1933.

(Right Lower)
BRISTOL TITAN SCHOOL MACHINE (1928)
Titan School Machine with competition number 20 on tail fin and direct drive Bristol *Titan* engine at Filton prior to being flown in the 1928 King's Cup Air Race.

G-EBGA
G

20

(Above)
BRISTOL FIGHTER mk.II (1921)
The F2B mk.II was also known as the "J-type" after the prototype J6586 shown here. 435 Fighters were rebuilt to F2B mk.II as the standard Army co-operation biplane in the early 1920's.

(Below)
BRISTOL F2B 300H.S. (1924)
***G-EBCN* with 300hp Hispano-Suiza engine was sold to SABCA (Spain) in 1924 with fifteen similar airframes.**

(Above)
BRISTOL JUPITER FIGHTER (1923)
A Bristol Fighter converted to take a *Jupiter* engine, *G-EBGF* was the first of three similar machines. It crashed in November 1923 and was finally scrapped in April 1925.

(Below)
BRISTOL JUPITER FIGHTER (1924)
G-EBHG in Sweden in 1924 during Arctic trials.
The second of the three Jupiter Fighters was rebuilt with carburetor heating and other modifications to make it suitable for use in Arctic temperatures

After demonstration it was sold to the Swedish Army on 6 May 1924 and was used until about 1935 when it was sold to a private buyer for further use.

(Above)
BRISTOL JUPITER SCHOOL MACHINE (1924)
G-EBIH the first of the initial batch of seven School Machines in 1924. First flown on 5 July 1924 it was written off after a mid air collision with Lucifer School Machine *G-EBGB* on 20 August 1929.

(Right Upper)
BRISTOL FIGHTER 'C' (1923)
Prototype Fighter 'C' as built with small tail fin and Frise ailerons on both upper and lower wings.
The Fighter 'C' was devised as a successor to the ubiquitous F2B and used a 436hp Bristol *Jupiter V* engine.

(Right Centre)
BRISTOL BLOODHOUND (1924)
The Bristol Fighter C was rebuilt with a larger rudder and metal wings having increased sweep-back and, registered *G-EBGG,* was officially named Bloodhound.

(Right Lower)
BRISTOL BLOODHOUND (1925)
J7237 the second Air Ministry owned Bloodhound with Jupiter engine and wooden wings on 18 August 1925.
Three Bloodhounds similar to the prototype *G-EBGG* were built in 1925 and sold to the Air Ministry for trials. All had tubular steel fuselages covered with doped fabric but only the third machine *J7248* had metal wings — the other two having wooden ones. They were tested at Martlesham Heath and Farnborough but a production order did not follow.

(Below)
BRISTOL JUPITER SCHOOL MACHINE (1926-31)
G-EBOC at Filton when new in 1926.
A second batch of Jupiter engined School Machines was built from 1926 which had plywood covered fuselages to make them more durable. *G-EBOC* was the first of 14 machines and was used at the flying school at Filton until it collided with a similar trainer *G-AAWJ* on 7 July 1931.

G-EBGG
G

True to Type

One relatively minor change occurred in 1924 involving the designation of aircraft types. Hitherto, it had been the custom to use letters based on the aircraft name or description, for example, GB75, TTA, J10S etc. From 1924 a system of type numbers was employed whether a design was built or not. Previous designs were numbered in retrospect, but unfortunately for the historian, there was some bias because type 1 was given to the first Barnwell production design rather than the first Challenger Biplane of 1910 — over 200 aircraft being totally ignored. Incidentally, Bristol Tramways adopted a system of type identification at the same time but used letters instead of numbers to prevent confusion.

The first aircraft to be given a type number at the outset was the type 90 Berkeley which, contrary to the previous order of things, had been devised by Reid and concluded by Barnwell. The Berkeley was a two seater biplane bomber and three prototypes were built for Ministry testing and approval. *J7403* had wooden wings and was first flown on 5 March, 1925. It was followed by the second machine *J7404* also with wooden wings and in 1926 by *J7405* with metal wings. All three had Rolls Royce *Condor* water cooled engines and were accepted for trials but a production order was not forthcoming.

The Brownie was Captain Barnwell's design for the Light Aeroplane Competition of 1924 and was a low wing monoplane powered by a Bristol *Cherub* 2-cylinder engine. Three were built and flown by various flying clubs but the type 91 proved to be too expensive to make and not robust enough for the treatment given to it by learners.

The type 92 was a research aircraft built under an Air Ministry contract to relate the results of wind tunnel testing to actual fying experience. A two-seater, it was powered by a Bristol *Jupiter VI* engine and the intention was to alter the diameter of the fuselage to study the cooling problems of large air cooled radial engines. It flew as a development hack for about three years before it was finally abandoned.

Built as a speculative venture, the Boarhound type 93 was designed as a successor to the F2B army co-operation fighter and was first flown by Cyril Uwins on 8 June 1925. It had a steel framework incorporating a new design wing having steel ribs in place of aluminium as used in the Bloodhound.

The Beaver type 93A was a development of the Boarhound to meet an Air Ministry specification for a general purpose biplane. It had a larger tailplane for improved stability, a more streamlined nose and extra ailerons on the upper wing. First flight was achieved on 23 February 1927 and later, with the civil registration *G-EBQF,* it took part in trials at Martlesham against other makes but was not ordered into production. Two aircraft of similar design named Boarhound II were sold to the Mexican Government in 1928.

Built as a 3 seat fighter armed with shell firing Coventry Ordnance Works (C.O.W.) guns, the type 95 Bagshot used two 450hp *Jupiter VI* engines and first flew in July 1927. It later proved to be unstable in flight and as the behaviour of large monoplane wings was not fully understood at the time the Bagshot was used for an extensive series of structural tests of its wings until the early 1930's when it was scrapped.

(Below)
BRISTOL TYPE 90 BERKELEY (1925)
First of the three Berkeley prototypes, *J7403* at Filton and as built with wooden wings. Having a 650hp Rolls Royce *Condor* engine the type 90 could carry 500lb of bombs and was armed with one fixed Vickers gun and a Scarff ring mounted Lewis gun.

(Right Upper)
BRISTOL TYPE 91 BROWNIE (1924)
Single seat Brownie *G-EBJM* at Filton in 1924.
The third Brownie, a single seater, had metal wings of 30ft-7in span and first flew on 24 September 1924. It was flown into second place by Cyril Uwins in the 1926 Grosvenor Cup air race finally passing to the London Aero Club where it was in use regularly until about 1930 when it was scrapped.

(Above)
BRISTOL TYPE 91A BROWNIE (1925)
Brownie *G-EBJK* in its intermediate form at Filton in 1925.
The first of the three Brownie's had a chequered career. *G-EBJK* was first flown as a type 91 on 6 August 1924 with wooden wings of 34ft-7in span and a Bristol *Cherub I* engine.
It was later modified to type 91A with a Bristol *Cherub III* engine and metal wings of 37ft-7in span for official trials.
A further modification to type 91B, Brownie II occured in 1926 and it was flown in competitions of that year gaining a third and a second prize. Frank Barnwell crashed it at Farnborough in 1928 and it was written off.

(Below)
BRISTOL TYPE 92 LABORATORY MACHINE (1925)
The Laboratory biplane inside the Experimental Flight Shed at Patchway in 1925 before the installation of the engine.
Different diameter fairings could be added to the fuselage to study the cooling of air cooled radial engines.

G-EBLG

(Left Upper)
BRISTOL TYPE 93 BOARHOUND (1925)
Boarhound mk.I with 425hp *Jupiter* engine when new in 1925. *G-EBLG* was rebuilt after being crashed by a RAF pilot and was used for development work.

(Left Centre)
BRISTOL TYPE 93A BEAVER (1927)
G-EBQF with Bristol Jupiter engine as-built in 1927. Similar to the Boardhound from which it was derived the Beaver had a different tail and front fuselage. Two biplanes known as Boarhound II were sold to Mexico but it is not clear whether they were new machines or rebuilds of *G-EBLG* and *G-EBQF.*

(Left Lower)
BRISTOL TYPE 95 BAGSHOT (1927)
The sole prototype Bagshot, *J7767,* in the late 1920's during structural testing of its wings in the hangar now used by Rolls Royce and adjacent to the A38 overpass.
Originally called Bludgeon, the type 95 had two *Jupiter* engines, two 37mm C.O.W. guns and carried a crew of three.

(Below)
BRISTOL FIGHTER MK.III TYPE 96 (1926)
New F2B mk.II army co-operation fighter *J8251* at Filton in 1926.

(Bottom)
BRISTOL FIGHTER MK.IV TYPE 96A (1927)
J8250, one of the dual control versions of the F2B mk.IV. Converted from mk.II or mk.III Fighters, the mk.IV had a larger tail and Handley Page auto slots on the upper wing. Filton was not involved to any great extent in the rebuilding of these.

A strengthened version of the F2B was produced from 1926 which was outwardly similar to previous marks and used the 275hp R.R. *Falcon III* engine. Eighty-three type 96 machines including 31 dual control types were built in 1925/27 and large numbers of earlier F2B's were reconditioned and converted to mk.III standard.

The Fighter mk.IV type 96A introduced in 1927 was a further strengthened form of the mk.III and was distinguished by the enlarged tail-fin and rudder and by the Handley-Page auto slots on the outer leading edge of the upper wing. All mk.IV machines were conversions of earlier mk.II and mk.III Fighters and most of the work was done by the RAF.

One Badminton, seq.6921, was built in 1926 purely as a racing machine in the hope of gaining added prestige for the *Jupiter* engine by winning the King's Cup Air Race. It was entered in the 1926 race but had to retire due to fuel starvation. After the race the type 99 was modified to improve the pilot's view by removing the fairing between the fuselage and the top wing. In this form it was used for test flying of the new Bristol *Orion* engine.

For the second attempt at winning the King's Cup, the Badminton was rebuilt with wider, tapered, wings separated by a faired steel strut. A smaller diameter 525hp short-stroke *Jupiter* enclosed by a modified cowling was also installed and it was recorded as type 99A. Unfortunately, while being tested on 28 July 1927 it stalled due to engine seizure and crashed in a field near Winterbourne killing the pilot, Capt. Barnard.

A two seat fighter biplane, the type 101 had steel wings but with a wooden fuselage and was propelled by a Jupiter engine, *G-EBOW* was used as a hack for flight testing of the *Jupiter VI* engine but was flown into second place in the 1928 King's Cup Air Race by Cyril Uwins. Although not put into production, the 101 was useful apart from engine trials, in the development of the Bristol steel strip method of construction used so successfully in the subsequent Bulldog fighter.

The most famous Bristol aeroplane of the 1920-1934 period must undoubtedly be the type 105 Bulldog which first flew on 17 May 1927. It was followed on 21 January 1928 by the maiden flight of the Bulldog mk.II which had a longer tail for improved stability. Production deliveries of mk.II's to the RAF commenced in 1929 and 129 had been produced by 1930 including those sold to Latvia, Siam, U.S. Navy, Australia, Sweden and Esthonia.

Forged cylinder heads were introduced on F-series *Jupiters* in 1929 and with *Jupiter VIIF* engine the Bulldog became mk.IIA. The Bulldog was a stable production line and 262 Bulldog IIA's were sold to the RAF between 1931 and 1934 plus a Company demonstrator *R11* (later registered *G-ABBB)* and an experimental airframe made of stainless steel.

Production was set to continue with the *Mercury*-engined Bulldog IIIA but unfortunately the RAF preferred the Gloster *Gauntlet* instead and only two mk.IIIA's were actually built and flown in 1931/2. The prototype with the marking *R5* was used for *Mercury* development until it crashed in March 1933, while the second, *R7,* was converted to a mk.IVA prototype. *R8,* another mk.IVA was built as a demonstrator but used as a flying test bed for the new Bristol *Perseus* sleeve valve engine.

In 1929 a bare Bulldog airframe (7341) was sent to Japan and that Government asked Bristol to design a version suitable for manufacture in Japan. Two aircraft known as the Bulldog type 105J Japanese Single Seat Fighter were built in Japan and successfully flown with licence built *Jupiters.* However, an order for further aircraft under a licencing agreement was not forthcoming.

The last Bulldogs were a batch of 17 mk.IVA's built to the special requirements of the Finnish Air Force in 1934/35 and one of these (serial *BU59*) is preserved in Finland.

(Below)
BRISTOL TYPE 99 BADMINTON I (1926)
G-EBMK as built in 1926 but with the streamlined cylinder helmets and spinner removed.

(Right)
BRISTOL TYPE 99A BADMINTON II (1927)

G-EBMK **as rebuilt with tapered wings and faired interplane struts for the 1927 King's Cup Air Race. Capt.F.L.Barnard was killed while practising on 28 July 1927.**

(Centre)
BRISTOL TYPE 101 (1927)

Type 101 at Filton in 1927 and in original condition with forward firing guns between the cylinders in addition to a Scarff ring mounted rear gun.

(Bottom)
BRISTOL TYPE 105 BULLDOG mk.II (1928)

K1085 **was one of a batch of 23 Bulldog II single seat fighters built for the RAF in 1930.**

The production version of the Bulldog was known as the type 105 mk.II and of the 129 to be built most went to RAF squadrons between 1928 and 1930. The mk.II was 2ft longer and had marginally better performance than the mk.I but retained the 440hp Bristol *Jupiter* engine. *(Aeroplane photo)*

R8

(Left Upper)
BRISTOL TYPE 105 BULLDOG mk.II (1929)
Bulldog mk.II for Latvia at Filton in the years before the swastika device was made a sign of hatred by Adolf Hitler.
Five Bulldogs were supplied to Latvia in 1929 with licence-built French Gnome-Rhone *Jupiter* engines and Oerliken guns. A second batch of seven machines followed in 1930.

(Left Centre)
BRISTOL TYPE 105 BULLDOG mk.IVA (1933)
Bulldog mk.IVA bearing class B mark *R8* as exhibited at the SBAC show in June 1934.
***R8,* the second Bulldog IVA was used for flight testing of the new Bristol *Perseus* sleeve valve engine. It first flew in the autumn of 1933 and crashed in February 1934 but was rebuilt as shown. In a later rebuilding it was fitted with a Bristol *Mercury* engine.**

(Left Lower)
BRISTOL TYPE 105D BULLDOG (1913)
Danish Bulldog at Filton in 1931 prior to delivery.
Four Bulldogs were built to the special requirements of the Danish Air Force. They had Bristol *Jupiter VIF.M* engines, Madsen gun gear in place of the usual Vickers armament, and survived until after the occupation of Denmark by the Nazis.

(Above)
BRISTOL TYPE 105J BULLDOG JSSF (1930)
The first of two Japanese Single Seat Fighters to be built in Tokyo in 1930.

Built as a single seat interception fighter with maximum rate of climb for interception by sight without radio, the Bullpup was similar to the type 105 Bulldog albeit a little smaller. Only one type 107 prototype was ordered and registered *J9051.* Although the property of the Air Ministry it was used by the Company for development of the Bristol *Mercury* and other engines. It first flew with a *Jupiter* engine in April 1928 but was subsequently flown with *Mercury,* short-stroke *Mercury* and *Aquila* engines.

G-EBZK was a large single engined biplane built especially for very long range flying with a view to capturing the World Distance Record. It was designed for a range of 5000 miles at an economical cruising speed of 90mph and a take off weight of 9800lb. It first flew in September 1928. When it was realised that the type 109 was unlikely to fulfil its original role by a comfortable margin it was used in 1930 for flight testing of the *Jupiter* engine under an Air Ministry contract and was dismantled soon afterwards.

The type 110A Commercial Biplane first flew in October 1929 with a Bristol *Neptune* engine and was intended to be 4-passenger civil transport for overseas as well as U.K. use. It used existing Bulldog components, tooling and methods of manufacture where possible to produce a sturdy yet economically priced aircraft. It was damaged in a landing accident in February 1930 and was subsequently scrapped because of its poor sales prospects. A second airframe was not completed.

Two type 118 private venture prototypes were started in 1930/31 for the RAF and were 2 seat General Purpose Biplanes. The type 118 was designed to carry about 500lb of bombs, cameras or could be adapted as an air ambulance. The first one was flown in January 1931 but the second was not completed as type 118.

The type 120 was formerly the second type 118 prototype but had a transparent cupola to protect the rear gunner from the slipstream. On its first flight in January 1932 it gave a top speed of 165mph at 1200ft and an initial rate of climb exceeding 1000ft per minute. As *R6* it was purchased by the Air Ministry in 1933 and as *K3587* was used for testing of the secret cupola in flying conditions.

The last biplane to be designed at Filton, but not the last to be built, was a private venture for an Air Ministry competition for a high performance single seat fighter having four Vickers guns in the nose. A Rolls Royce *Goshawk III* engine gave it a very sleek appearance but problems with its evaporative cooling system caused delays. The type 123 was found to be unstable during its first flight in June 1934 and further development was abandoned in favour of the type 133 monoplane.

A two seat version of the Bulldog was introduced in 1931 for advanced training and was known as the type 124 or Bulldog T.M. Sixty aircraft were produced for the RAF between 1932 and 1934. The last of these, sequence no.7837, was the last Bristol designed biplane to be built at Filton.

The Bulldog T.M. was not, however, the last biplane to be made at Filton. 141 Hawker *Audax* biplanes were built at Filton for the RAF in 1935/36 becoming the last of the old breed to leave the Works. Mention should also be made here of another foreign biplane. Earlier, in the years 1928 to 1930, Filton had also built 84 Armstrong Whitworth *Siskin IIIA* fighters for the RAF and reconditioned 15 others. So ended a most difficult chapter in the BAC history yet what it lacked in big orders it certainly made up for in variety.

(Below)
BRISTOL TYPE 107 BULLPUP (1928)
The Bullpup prototype in one of its many forms with Bristol *Aquila* sleeve valve engine and as flown at the 1935 Show organised by the Society of British Aviation Constructors.

(Bottom)
BRISTOL TYPE 109 LONG RANGE MACHINE (1928)
Bearing the registration *G-EBZK* and class B mark *R2* at the same time the Long Range Biplane is seen during endurance testing of a sealed Bristol *Jupiter XIF* engine in September 1930.

(Above)
BRISTOL TYPE 110A COMMERCIAL BIPLANE (1929)
The sole type 110A, *G-AAFG,* with Bristol *Neptune* engine at Filton in January 1930.

(Below)
BRISTOL TYPE 118 GENERAL PURPOSE MACHINE (1930)
Looking like a relic from prehistoric times, the first type 118 as bare bones at Filton in 1930. It was of all metal construction and had a *Jupiter XF* engine.

(Above)

BRISTOL TYPE 118 GENERAL PURPOSE MACHINE (1930)

The first type 118 prototype general purpose Service land plane with the marking *R3* in flight in June 1931.

***R3 (G-ABEZ)* first flew in January 1931 with Bristol *Mercury XFA* motor but this was later replaced by a *Mercury V*. The second type 118 prototype was redesigned during construction and became type 120.** *(Flight photo).*

(Below)

BRISTOL TYPE 120 GENERAL PURPOSE MACHINE (1932)

Type 120 G.P. Machine with marking *R6,* modified cupola and 650hp *Pegasus II* engine in 1932. The 'Parrot cage' was hand operated and was Bristols first venture in turret design. In 1935 an Armaments Division was formed to develop power operated turrets.

(Above)
BRISTOL TYPE 123 FOUR GUN FIGHTER (1934)
Type 123 at Filton when new. Powered by a Rolls Royce ***Goshawk*** engine and with four .303 Vickers guns, the type 123 was very much a ''If you can't beat 'em join 'em'' design using the increasingly popular water cooled in-line engine instead of the air cooled Bristol radial.

(Below)
BRISTOL TYPE 124 BULLDOG T.M. (1931)
K3170 was the first of the production version of the Bulldog Training Machine with two cockpits having dual controls and was powered by a Bristol ***Jupiter*** engine.

Limited Yet Unlimited

Under the terms of the Treaty of Versailles, signed in 1919, Germany was prevented from building aeroplanes or indeed any other form of war material. There was a slight relaxation in 1922 when the manufacture of civil aircraft was permitted but the machines were restricted in weight, engine power, speed, range and altitude. Later in 1926 the training of up to ten pilots per year was permitted for civilian duties only. Also in 1926 the German national carrier Lufthansa was formed and was to play an important role in the resurgence of Germany.

The deep resentment felt in high places over the defeat of Germany in 1918 was compounded by the humiliation of the German people by the terms of the Treaty. Despite all the restrictions the more aggressive military leaders set out to circumvent the Treaty and to re-arm the German forces. Lufthansa was used secretively to train air crews in readiness for a revival of the German air force at an appropriate time.

Adolf Hitler came to power in 1933 at the head of the National Socialist Party after the enforced collapse of the democratic government. Hitler's intended aim to expand the German empire and his expressed belief that the events of 1918 were only a temporary set back was supported by the new military hierarchy that he had created.

The placing of massive orders in 1933 for hundreds of new aircraft initiated rapid expansion of the dormant German aircraft industry. Dornier, Heinkel, Focke-Wulf, Junkers and Messerschmitt built and equipped large factories backed up by substantial research organisations.

In the spring of 1935 the civilian masquerade was dropped and the full might of the Luftwaffe revealed to the World. At this juncture the new German air force had at its disposal almost 2000 aircraft of various forms and ten times that many men to operate them.

At home, meanwhile, the Depression was taking its toll of manufacturing firms and combined with the efforts of a vociferous minority of pacifists to restrict military spending the RAF was equipped with obsolescent aircraft.

It was transparently obvious even before the unveiling of the Luftwaffe that Hitler was amassing a lot of military hardware and it was inevitable that someone, somewhere, was going to get a 'hiding'. At the risk of being branded warmongers the more enlightened political leaders could foresee the danger and a full programme of rearmament was embarked upon.

The British aircraft industry expanded rapidly to keep pace with the threat from across the English Channel; the Bristol Aeroplane Company being no exception. On 15 June 1935 the Company was reformed as a public limited company with a share capital of £1,200,000.

During the next half-decade the Filton Works was

(Below)
The main gate at the Filton Works in 1939 with the camouflaged new Filton House on the left and the machine shop in the background.

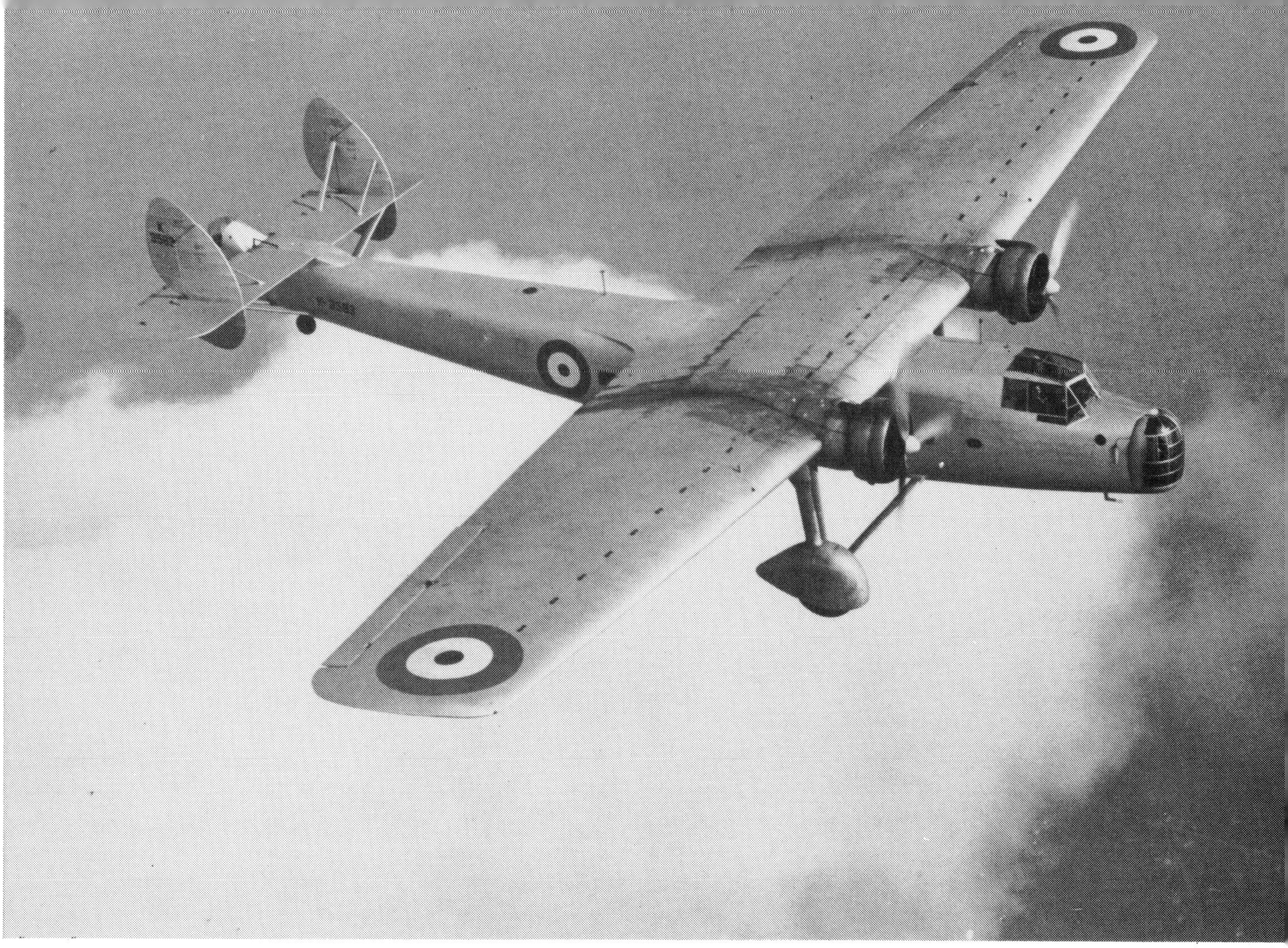

(Above)
BRISTOL TYPE 130 (1935)
Prototype type 130 in flight in 1935.

The type 130 was a descendant of the Bagshot fighter and was built to meet an Air Ministry specification for an aircraft to carry 24 troops or mixed freight.

It was a high wing monoplane having a steel strip and aluminium frame covered by a stressed Alclad skin. Two Bristol Pegasus engines were used and *K3583* was first flown in June 1935. It remained at Filton as a development machine until the early 1940's. (*Flight photo.*)

(Below)
BRISTOL TYPE 130A BOMBAY (1939)
L5808 the first of fifty Bombays at Queen's Island, Belfast in 1939.

Production of the type 130 was undertaken by Short Brothers and Harland in Northern Ireland because Filton was fully stretched with production of the Blenheim. Their all metal construction made them suitable for operation in the Far East where they gave valuable, if unglamorous, service in the Second War.

expanded to cope with large orders for new aircraft. The floor area of the Erecting Hall (now MPS) was doubled, a new toolroom and a metal store were built and the machine shop in the former bus sheds was further extended. For the building of wings a new main plane assembly shop was also built (now S68 toolroom).

In addition to the expansion 'up the hill' a new 200,000 square feet engine factory was built on the opposite side of the road from the Flying School hangars and extending towards the GWR railway line.

1935 was an important year in the history of BAC for besides the reorganisation and expansion it roughly coincided with a radical change in methods of aeroplane construction. Enough knowledge existed by this time about the behaviour of monoplane wings to allow the retirement of the 'belts and braces' biplane which had been the front line machine for twenty years and more.

Airframe design had taken great strides since the Great War. Wood as a structural material was definitely out and steel imposed severe weight penalties. Duralumin, an alloy of aluminium with up to 4% copper, was being used successfully in a small way but suffered from corrosion if not suitably protected from the elements. The American invention of Alclad, in which duralumin is coated with a thin film of pure aluminium, together with new techniques for the heat treatment of higher strength structural aluminium alloys completely changed construction methods. The

(Above)
BRISTOL TYPE 133 (1934)
Type 133 monoplane, as rebuilt with cockpit canopy and small ailerons, bearing the mark *R10* at Filton in September 1934.
Built as a private venture the type 133 monoplane was intended to meet the same F7/30 specification as the type 123 biplane. It was a single seat fighter of all metal construction with a Bristol Mercury IVS.2 engine. This promising aircraft was lost when, during flight testing, it crashed in an orchard at Longwell Green. The pilot took to the silk and survived. (*Flight photo*).

(Below)
BRISTOL TYPE 138A ALTITUDE MACHINE (1936)
Type 138A monoplane *K4879* at Farnborough in 1936. Designed especially for an attempt on the World Altitude Record, the type 138A first flew in May 1936 with a Bristol Pegasus IV engine. Later, with a special supercharged Pegasus engine it climbed to a record height of 53,937 feet. It continued to be used for research at very high altitude but a second machine, type 138B, was not flown. (*Flight photo*).

(Above)
BRISTOL TYPE 142 BRITAIN FIRST (1935)
The type 142 as originally built carrying the experimental mark *R-12;* it was later registered *K7557.*
A low wing commercial monoplane with 2 Bristol Mercury VIS2 engines, the type 142 could carry a crew of a 2 plus 4 passengers. It was built to the order of Lord Rothemere, *Daily Mail* proprietor and aviation enthusiast, who named it Britain First before presenting it to the Nation. From it was derived a military version type 142M; the Blenheim.

doped-fabric covered space frame concept gave way to stressed-skin monocoque structures but not without problems.

The first Bristol machines to have stressed-skin aluminium airframes were the type 133 monoplane fighter of 1933 and the type 130 which appeared in prototype form in 1932. The type 138A Altitude Machine on the other hand was a special purpose machine with a wood and metal airframe for minimum weight.

Britain First

In 1934 Bristol had proposed a small low-wing cabin monoplane, type 135, having two Bristol *Aquila* engines and capable of a top speed of about 180mph.

Lord Rothermere's involvement in the building of the subsequent type 142 has been well chronicled elsewhere so suffice it to say that he was impressed by the type 135 project and ordered a variant of it. The type 142 was a low wing cabin monoplane with two Bristol *Mercury* engines which gave it better performance than the type 135 could have had. It had an all-metal monocoque fuselage built up of transverse frames and longerons covered with a flush riveted Alclad skin. The three part wing was built on two steel spars and pressed light alloy ribs with an Alclad skin. Five passengers could be accommodated in addition to the crew of two.

First flown in the spring of 1935 with the experimental mark *R12,* the type 142 was presented to the Nation in July after being christened *Britain First* by Lord Rothemere as an example of a good modern aeroplane. It was put through its official trials bearing the registration *K7557* achieving a maximum speed of 285mph which surpassed that of the RAF's front line fighters.

Built at the same time as the Britain First, the multi-

(Below)
BRISTOL TYPE 143 (1936)
Prototype type 143 at Filton in July 1936 with wooden airscrews and experimental mark *R-14.*
The type 143 was a multi-purpose low wing passenger monoplane derived from the type 142 Britain First with 2 Bristol Aquila engines. It was used as a flying test bed for the new Aquila 9-cylinder radial engine but this was abandoned in 1938 and the airframe was scrapped several years later.

purpose monoplane type 143 was an alternative form of the type 142 using Bristol *Aquila* engines as proposed for the type 135 project. It was a low wing monoplane of all metal construction with a longer fuselage that could seat eight passengers and a crew of two.

With the experimental mark *R14* the type 143 first flew in January 1936 being used subsequently as a flying test bed for the *Aquila* engine. Enquiries were received for the type 143 from home and overseas customers but these had to be declined due to the heavy committment to the bomber version of the type 142 — the now famous Blenheim.

Blenheim

The type 142M Blenheim was a direct development of the *Britain First* but with a mid-wing arrangement to enable the internal stowage of a 1000lb bomb load. Its twin Bristol *Mercury* engines gave it a range of 1000 miles and a top speed approaching 300mph.

K7033, the prototype Blenheim first flew on 25 June 1936 piloted by C.F. Uwins and deliveries of production machines commenced in March 1937. In addition to the 634 'short nosed' Blenheim I's delivered to the RAF, others were exported or built under licence.

Eighteen machines were delivered to Finland in 1937 and were later joined by a further 45 Blenheim I's built by Valtion, Finland under a licencing agreement. The Government of Jugoslavia also arranged for Blenheims to be built under licence by Ikarus. Two Blenheims were flown out to Jugoslavia bearing registrations *G-AFCE* and *G-AFCF* for use as patterns for the guidance of the local workforce. Sixteen machines were built there and flown but another 24 were destroyed when the factory was sabotaged by patriots to prevent it falling into German hands. The Turkish Government purchased thirty Filton-built Blenheim I's which were delivered with British civil markings excepting the first two which were crated for transport by sea.

Licence agreements with British firms resulted in 250 machines being built by A.V. Roe at Chadderton and 422 built by Rootes Securities at Speke in Liverpool. A total of 1457 Blenheim I's were eventually built including 700 at Filton. Some of these machines were later modified with a longer nose and longer range to become the Blenheim IV.

In 1939 a proposal was submitted for a general reconnaissance version of the Blenheim for RAF Coastal Command having a longer nose for a forward navigators' position and known as the type 149 Bolingbroke. A production 142M machine *K7072* was modified as a prototype Bolingbroke and an order for 134 production Bolingbrokes was received but was later withdrawn. This prototype was subsequently known as Blenheim mk.III.

The aborted Bolingbroke project developed into the Blenheim IV multi-purpose machine which had the nose extended by 3ft, larger fuel tanks, armour plating, a chin turret under the nose to protect the vulnerable belly of the aircraft and twin-gun dorsal turret for top side protection. More powerful Bristol *Mercury XV* engines were installed.

The Blenheim IV replaced the Blenheim I in production in late summer 1939 but in the event only 312 mk.IV machines were built at Filton before the line was closed down to make space for the new Beaufighter.

Work on the Blenheim IV was transferred to shadow factories where 750 were built by A.V.Roe and 2060 by Rootes. Overseas, 15 machines were built by Valtion, Finland and 12 Filton built machines were exported to Greece.

Licence production of the Blenheim IV was also undertaken in Canada by Fairchild, Quebec under the revived name Bolingbroke. The Canadian machines were built to suit the cold Arctic climate and could operate on wheels, skis, or floats. Bolingbroke I machines were powered by two 840hp Bristol *Mercury VIII* engines while a solitary mark II variant used two

(Below)
BRISTOL TYPE 142M BLENHEIM I (1937)
Early short nosed Blenheim I built at Filton in 1937 but later converted to Blenheim mk1F night fighter and fitted with A.I. mk.3 radar.

750hp Pratt & Whitney *Twin Wasp Junior* engines. Bolingbroke IV's, the principal production form, were fitted with larger 920hp *Mercury XV* engines. A total of 676 Bolingbrokes of the three variants was produced by Fairchild for the Royal Canadian Air Force for the protection of the eastern coastline of Canada from Labrador to the Maritime Provinces.

Blenheim bombers served in France in 1939-40 and later carried out daylight raids over enemy held territory in which role the 1,900 miles range of the Blenheim IV was an advantage. In 1940 Blenheim mk.I and mk.IV machines were converted to fighters with the designation mk.IF and mk.IVF respectively. These had a battery of fixed guns under the nose and were used for long range bomber-escort duties and also as night fighters until replaced by the Beaufighter. Blenheims served overseas in the Mediterranean against the Nazis and the Far East to help stem the Japanese invasion.

(Bottom)
BRISTOL TYPE 149 BLENHEIM IV (1939)
The mk.IV was a development of the Blenheim mk.I with an extended nose, extra range, armour plating, undernose gun position and a twin-gun dorsal turret. 3137 were built at Filton or by A.V. Roe, Rootes or Valtion (Finland).

Blenheim V

Derived from the Blenheim IV, the type 160 was a close support and high altitude bomber with two Bristol *Mercury* engines. Two prototypes were built at Filton and were named Bisley. The first, *AD657* was an armoured two seat dive bomber with a twin-gun dorsal turret while *AD661,* the second prototype was arranged as a high altitude day bomber. *AD657* first flew on 24 February 1941.

Production of the Bisley was undertaken by Rootes at Blythe Bridge, Staffs after the last Blenheim IV had been completed and was built on the same jigs.

(Below)
BRISTOL TYPE 142M (1937)
Blenheim mk.1 from the first production batch delivered to the RAF in 1937.

Developed from the type 142 Britain First, the 142M Blenheim was a mid wing bomber with two Bristol Mercury VIII engines. The mk.1 was the original short nosed production machine and was capable of a top speed of 282mph at 15,000ft with a bomb load of 1,000lb.

Conversions were made to mk.1F which had a battery of fixed guns in a trough below the fuselage. 1,457 were built at Filton or by shadow factories at Chadderton, Liverpool, Finland and Jugoslavia. (*Flight photo*).

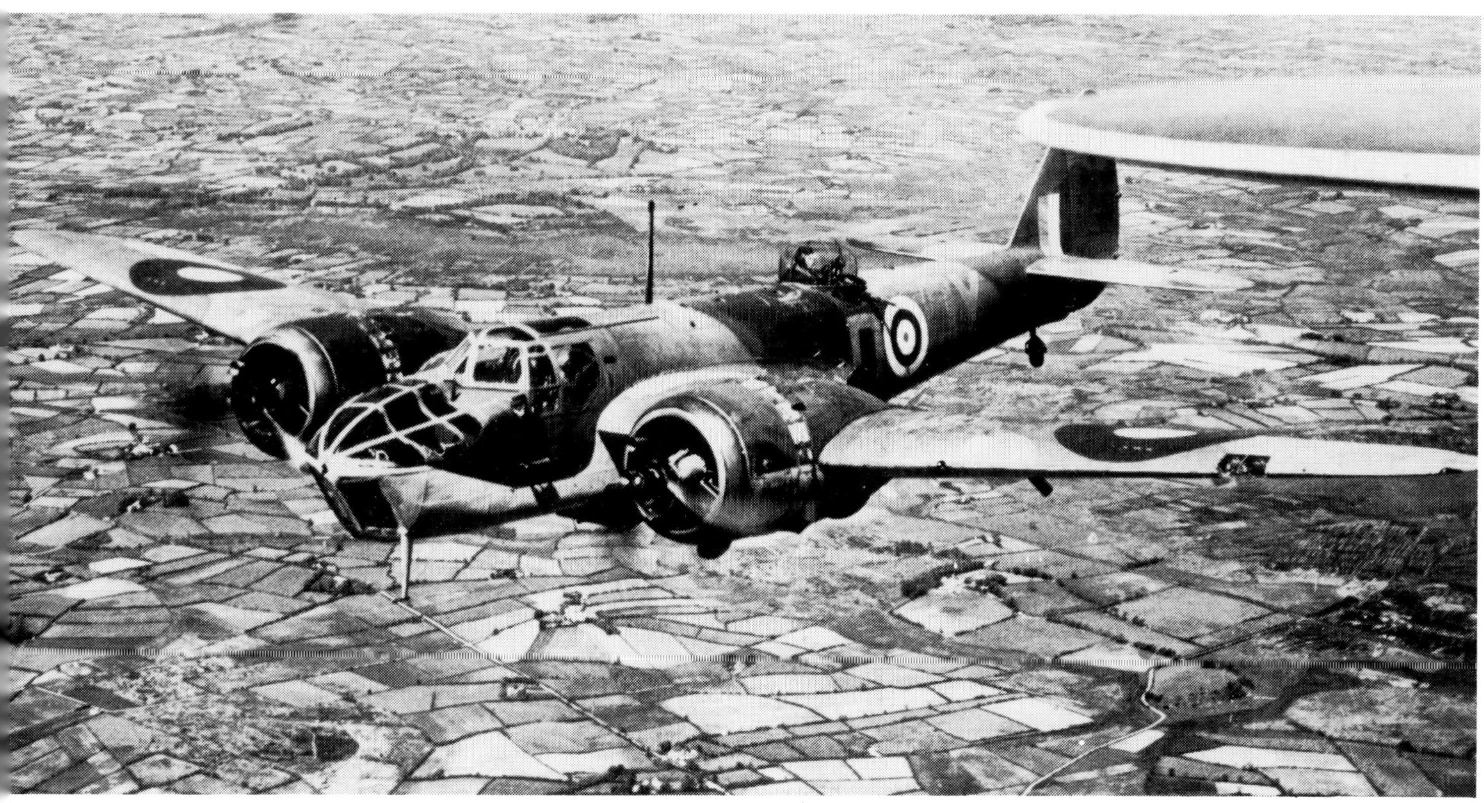

V6083
FV

L4842
L
4842
L4842

(Left Upper)
BRISTOL BLENHEIM IV (1939)
A classic portrait of "Long nose" Blenheim IV serial *V6083* showing the underside defence gun and the twin-gun Bristol dorsal turret. *(Flight photo)*

(Left Lower)
BRISTOL BLENHEIM IV.
L4842 was originally built as a "short nose" Blenheim and does not have the under-nose gun. *(Flight photo)*

(Above)
BRISTOL TYPE 149 BOLINGBROKE (1939)
The proposed type 149 Bolingbroke became the Blenheim IV but the name was later revived for a version of the Blenheim IV built in Canada by Fairchild. *9912* was a Bolingbroke mk.4.

(Below)
BRISTOL TYPE 149 BOLINGBROKE (1939)
Bolingbroke mk.III *no.717* with experimental installation of EDO floats in Quebec Province in 1939.

(Above)
BRISTOL TYPE 160 BISLEY (1942)
Second prototype Bisley, serial *no AD661*, at Filton in 1942.
Two prototype type 160 twin engined bombers were built and were the only machines to be named Bisley. Production was undertaken by Rootes and the type 160 was renamed Blenheim V by the Air Ministry.

(Right)
BRISTOL TYPE 160 BISLEY (1940)
First prototype Bisley, serial *AD657*, at Filton when new.

(Below)
BRISTOL TYPE 160 BLENHEIM V (1940)
A7030 was one of 942 Blenheim V's built by Rootes Securities with the distinctive sloping nose and navigators ''bath''.

Renamed Blenheim V, the type 160 was built in three production versions — three seat high altitude bomber, two seat low level close support bomber, and three seat advanced trainer. Only the low level bomber had the external armour plating around the crew positions and turret.

With a maximum speed of 266mph the Blenheim V was slower than the Blenheim IV and was found in service to be vulnerable to attack if the enemy fighter cover was good. Many Blenheim V's were outfitted for use in the tropics and found their way to Malaya and other Far East countries in the campaign against the Japanese. 942 type 160 Blenheim V's were built by Rootes.

Types 146 and 148

Bristol's most famous aeroplanes of the 1934-44 period were the twin-engined successors to the Britain First. Besides the type 138A Altitude Machine there were, however, other diversions into single-engined products.

Based on an Air Ministry specification issued in 1934, the type 146 was a single-seat fighter monoplane of similar size to the unfortunate type 133. It had an aluminium stressed-skin airframe and was armed with .303in Browning guns in the outer wings. At first it was proposed to use the Bristol *Perseus* engine but first flight was achieved on 11 February 1938 using a Bristol *Mercury* engine.

After Air Ministry trials it was returned to Filton but was damaged during a landing and was not repaired. A second airframe, works sequence number 7842, was not completed — the specification having been adequately fulfilled by the Rolls Royce engined Hawker Hurricane and Supermarine Spitfire.

Built at the same time as the type 146 and sharing similar methods of construction, the type 148 Army Cooperation monoplane was commenced in 1935. Three prototypes were ordered but only two were eventually built. The first, *K6551* with Bristol *Mercury* engine was flown for the first time on 15 October 1937 and showed itself capable of great flexibility of flying speeds from 62 to 255mph. It was later damaged in a 'wheels up' landing but was rebuilt and used for testing the Bristol *Perseus* sleeve valve engine after the demise of the type 146. *K6552* the second prototype (type 148B) was similarly used, after its maiden flight in May 1938, for flight testing of the Bristol *Taurus* engine.

The Westland *Lysander* with its high wing and superior visibility was chosen in preference to the type 148 but this was not a complete loss to Filton because the Lysander used the *Perseus* engine.

Beaufort

Also derived from the Blenheim, the type 152 Beaufort was a general reconnaissance and torpedo bomber having the torpedo half buried in the belly of the fuselage. It had two Bristol *Taurus* sleeve-valve radial engines and carried a crew of four. The upper portion of the fuselage over the wings was level

(Bottom)
BRISTOL TYPE 146 (1938)
The one and only type 146 monoplane, a prototype, at Filton in 1938.
the type 146 was a single seat fighter powered by a Bristol Perseus engine and was built to meet specification F5/34. It first flew on 11 Febraury 1938 but did not receive a production order and was scrapped after a landing accident in 1938.

(Bottom)
BRISTOL TYPE 148 (1937)
Mercury-engined first prototype in October 1937 at Filton.
Two type 148 Army Co-operation Monoplanes were built and flown in 1937/38 — *K6551* with a Mercury and *K6552* with a Bristol Taurus engine.

(Above)
BRISTOL TYPE 152 BEAUFORT (1937)
Beaufort mk.1's *N1172* and *L9834* on "patrol".
The Beaufort was a general reconnaissance and torpedo bomber with two Bristol Taurus sleeve valve engines. Over 2000 Beauforts of various marks were produced between 1937 and 1944 at Filton, Banwell and in Australia.

(Below)
BRISTOL TYPE 152 BEAUFORT mk.VIII (1943)
Australian built Beaufort *A9-700* the last of 700 Beaufort (mk.V to VIII) to be built down under.
They were used with the mk.IX conversions in the South Pacific to help counter the threat of the Japanese invasion.

between the cockpit and the twin gun dorsal turret giving the Beaufort its characteristic hump back profile.

First flight of the Beaufort took place on 15 October 1938, just after the untimely death of Frank Barnwell, and entered service in the spring of 1940. As well as being used against enemy shipping in the North Sea and the English Channel, the Beaufort saw active service over the Atlantic and Mediterranean.

1,429 Beaufort mk.I with *Taurus* engines and mk.II with Pratt & Whitney *Twin Wasp* engines were built between 1938 and 1944 at Filton and Banwell.

700 Beauforts of mk.V to mk.VIII were built in Australia with Pratt & Whitney *Twin Wasp* engines — the vast majority being mk.VIII produced from 1942 to 1944. Australian Beauforts were active against the Japanese in the Pacific and Far East.

Beaufighter

After several still-born schemes to fill a void in the inventory of the RAF for a fast cannon-armed fighter, Bristol evolved the type 156. A development of the Beaufort, the new fighter used as many production Beaufort parts as possible including the wings and tail unit. Existing Beaufort jigs were used to save time and for interchangeability of parts between the two aircraft types.

The first of four prototypes was completed in only six months and first flew on 17 July 1939, but another year was to elapse before the first machines were delivered to the RAF. After development flight testing the first Beaufighter prototype *R2052* was handed over to the RAF for evaluation on 2 April 1940, to be followed a couple of weeks later by the second prototype *R2053. R2052* with supercharged Bristol Hercules engines reached an estimated 335mph at 16,800ft but *R2053* with production *Hercules II* was disappointing at higher altitudes.

As the *Hercules III* engines specified for 300 production machines then on order were unlikely to give much improvement the Ministry pressed for alternative power plants to be considered. At first the choice lay between Bristol *Hercules IV* or Rolls Royce *Griffons* but as both these engines were still in the development stage it was decided to use the proven Rolls Royce *Merlin.* Machines with 1,400hp *Hercules* engines became known as Beaufighter mk.I, the *Merlin* engined version as mk.II while mk.III and mk.IV were reserved for a proposed type 158 'slim fuselage' Beaufighter with *Hercules IV* or *Griffons* respectively. The last mentioned pair were not built nor was the proposed bomber variant type 157.

The first ten production Beaufighters were delivered to the RAF in July and August 1940. By Spitfire and Hurricane standards the Beaufighter was rather large for a fighter but when an aircraft was required to carry the 1½ metre A.I. (Airborne Interception) mk.IV radar the Beaufighter was the only suitable machine available. Armed with four 20mm cannon in the nose, six Browning machine guns in the wings and radar the Beaufighter became the definitive RAF night fighter: a case of the right aircraft at the right time.

From the outset the Beaufighter was designed for unit construction so that it could be assembled from parts and sub assemblies made by various contractors. Shadow factories for Beaufighter production were set up by Fairey Aviation at Stockport, Cheshire; Ministry of Aircraft Production at Old Mixon, near Weston-Super-Mare (managed by Bristol), Rootes at Blythe Bridge, Staffs., and overseas in Victoria, Australia.

In the City of Bristol almost any building with a roof on was commandeered for shadow production of Beaufighter parts. When Bristol Tramways came under the control of the Ministry of Aircraft Production in 1940, the Motor Constructional Works at Brislington and many of the bus depots were used for the building of Beaufighter fuselages, nose and tail sub-assemblies,

(Above)
BRISTOL TYPE 156 BEAUFIGHTER 1F

Beaufighter 1F *R2198* from the sixth production batch delivered to RAF Fighter Command.

Beaufighters were given the suffix F or C to denote RAF Fighter or Coastal Commands respectively because each branch had different requirements. The mk.1 used 1,400hp Bristol Hercules sleeve valve radial engines and 915 mk.1 Beaufighters were built at Filton, Weston or Fairey Aviation before it was superseded by the mk.VI with more powerful engines.

wings, airscrews and armaments in general. Fuselages were transported from Brislington to Filton on an old bus chassis modified with a platform body and cradles. The partially finished Electricity House on the Centre and various garages were also acquired for shadow production.

The Beaufighter VI with more powerful 1,600hp *Hercules* engines became the production machine in 1941 after about 500 mk.I's had been built. Also in 1941, proposals were made to produce a torpedo fighter version of the Beaufighter to replace the Beaufort. This work culminated in the Beaufighter X with 1,734hp *Hercules* engines and an external torpedo rack. A contemporary variant without the torpedo release gear was known as Beaufighter XIC.

All Beaufighter X (also known as TF.X) and XIC machines were built by the shadow factories with 2205 TF.X and 163 XIC built before production ceased in 1945.

A version of the TF.X was built in Australia from microfilms sent from Filton; the first time this had been done. Australian Beaufighter XXI's were built after the completion of Beaufort orders with some 364 being produced between 1944 and 1945.

(Below)
BRISTOL TYPE 156 BEAUFIGHTER IIF (1941)
Filton built Beaufighter IIF *T3032* carrying encircled P marking to signify an unarmed prototype machine and the first type 156 with Rolls Royce engines.

Beaufighters with Rolls Royce Merlin XX engines were known as mark II and 448 were built at Filton but many were shipped as bare airframes due to late delivery of engines. To counter the extra length of the engine nacelles an enlarged dorsal fin was added to Merlin engined machines.

(Bottom)
BRISTOL TYPE 156 BEAUFIGHTER II (1941)
Beaufighter II *T3177* as flying test bed for the Rolls Royce Griffon engine in 1941.

The performance of the early Hercules engined Beaufighters was not up the expectations which prompted panic action by the Air Ministry to use Griffons. In the event the Bristol Hercules radial engine was improved and only a few Beaufighters received Griffons.

(Above)
BRISTOL TYPE 156 BEAUFIGHTER TF.X (1943)
LZ414 **taking off from Old Mixon where it was built.**
The Beaufighter TF.mk.X (Torpedo Fighter mark 10) was the ultimate form of the type 156 with 2095 built at Weston and 110 at Blythe Bridge. 163 machines known as Beaufighter XIc were similar but did not have torpedo gear.

(Below)
BRISTOL TYPE 156 BEAUFIGHTER TF.X (1944)
Beaufighter TF.X ***SR919,*** **the last aircraft to be built at the Weston factory in 1944 and with centimetric radar in the extended nose.**

Bombers

From 1934 the Bristol design team had proposed a succession of schemes for a heavy bomber in answer to specifications issued by the Air Ministry. Most did not get past the paper project stage but one did get as far as a mock up.

In 1938 Bristol submitted a proposal for a heavy bomber of 114ft wing span and 75ft long powered by four Bristol *Hercules VISM* supercharged engines. It was to have a range of 3,000 miles and be capable of a bomb load of 23,000lbs.

Specification B1-39 was issued and the design was revised to accommodate Bristol *Hercules* or Rolls Royce *Griffon* engines. In this form it resembled an enlarged four engine version of the Beaufort. A full scale wooden mock up was built in 1940 in the Experimental Shop (now Redux shop) and it was intended to build two prototypes. However, due to the imminent threat of invasion and Lord Beaverbrook's insistence on fighter production as a matter of great urgency, the project was dropped.

In 1940 Filton proposed a type 161 light bomber in reply to an Air Ministry specification. It was intended to take two forms — mk.I with *Hercules* engines and mk.II with Rolls Royce *Merlins.* The name Beaumont was provisionally allocated and the scheme evolved into the type 162 with two *Hercules* engines. A full scale mock up of the fuselage of the Beaumont was built in the Experimental Shop, alongside the type 159 Heavy Bomber, but was cancelled in favour of a new scheme for a Bristol *Centaurus* engined bomber, type 163.

After the Battle of Britain the RAF changed tactics from defensive to offensive with the result that large numbers of medium and heavy bombers were needed for night raids on German industrial targets.

Filton was instructed to disperse Beaufort and Beaufighter production to the shadow factories so that production of the new Buckingham could commence. The type 163 Buckingham was a mid wing medium bomber with two Bristol *Centaurus* 18-cylinder sleeve valve radial engines each developing 2,400hp. *DX249* the first of four prototypes flew in February 1943 and, after a few problems, about fifty production machines had been delivered by the end of 1944.

The Buckingham was designed on a unit system and was a very quick aeroplane to build from complete sub-assemblies built at various locations.

Unfortunately the needs of the RAF changed due to improved bombing techniques and the support of the United States Army Air Force with the consequence that the Buckingham was not needed. Only 119 production Buckinghams were actually built due to cancellations and at least half of these were built or delivered as Buckingham C.I fast courier transports. These were unarmed and had seats for four passengers with oxygen supply and had windows inserted into the sides. After the War the Buckingham was the basis of a proposed family of small airliners but the intended production did not happen.

(Below)

BRISTOL TYPE 163 BUCKINGHAM. (1943)

KV335 **was amongst the first batch of Buckingham B.1 twin Centaurus engined medium bombers to be delivered to the RAF in 1944.**

By the time that the Buckingham was in full production after many changes of official policy, the needs of War had changed and its usefulness diminished. Many were converted to unarmed light courier transports for four passengers in addition to a crew of three to become Buckingham C.1. A total of 123 were built but, after the War, many were scrapped without much flying time to their credit.

BRISTOL TYPE 164 BRIGAND B.1 (1945)

Brigand *RH754* of the second production batch with four rocket projectiles under each wing and a torpedo in the fuselage rack.

Almost 150 three seat Brigands were built in four basic forms; TF.1-Torpedo Fighter, B.1-Fighter Bomber, MET. 3-Meteorological reconnaissance and T.4-Radar Trainer.

Brigands came too late to see much active service in the Second War but were useful in a peace-keeping role in the Far East in the late 1940's and early 1950's.

Brigand

The adaptation of the Beaufighter as a torpedo bomber/fighter was successful but yet was not as good as an aeroplane built for the job would have been. Consequently, in 1942, Bristol set out a design for a *Hercules* engined torpedo bomber along similar lines to the Beaufighter but with a high set tail plane and bubble canopy. The Ministry issued specification H7/42 and a full scale wooden mock up of the fuselage was built in the Experimental Shop (now Redux) in 1942.

After considering alternative ideas a new machine was devised by using the H7/42 fuselage married to Buckingham style wings and tail with 2,500hp Bristol *Centaurus* engines as prime movers. The prototype of the new torpedo fighter christened type 164 Brigand, *MX988,* flew in December 1944.

By the time that the first eleven production Brigand TF.I had been delivered the War in Europe was over so the following 107 machines were built as Brigand B.I light bombers for use in the Far East. Most of these were delivered after Japan had surrendered and as late as 1948 for operation against Malayan terrorists.

Twenty-six machines went to the RAF as an unarmed meteorological reconnaissance variant Brigand MET.3 and finally, nine Brigand T.4 were delivered in 1950 as radar trainers with blacked out rear cockpits.

Buckmaster

To meet a need for a dual-control trainer, the type 166 Buckmaster was evolved which was a Buckingham having a wider front fuselage to seat a crew of two side-by-side.

Two Buckingham airframes were converted to become Buckmaster prototypes and the first was flown in October 1944. These were followed by 100 Buckmasters built from Buckingham components; a final order for ten being cancelled. Buckmasters were used at Operational Training Units for conversion training of pilots for the Brigand and Buckingham.

100 Ton Bomber

After the cancellation of the type 159 heavy bomber project the Filton Design Office kept apace with bomber development. In 1942 it was proposed to build a very large bomber of up to 225,000lbs total weight having a range of 5,000 miles. At least four schemes were considered including alternative vee and conventional tail surfaces. One scheme proposed using eight Bristol *Centaurus* engines coupled in pairs and driving contra-rotating pusher airscrews.

Such an advanced project as this would have been unlikely to see service before the War ended so the Air Ministry took the practical step of ordering more Lancasters instead.

Tempest

Towards the latter part of the War Bristol was given an order for about 500 Hawker Tempest II fighters with Bristol *Centaurus* engines — a design bearing some similarity to the Bristol type 133. With the ending of the War the contract was cancelled after 60 aircraft had been built at Banwell.

(Below)

BRISTOL TYPE 166 BUCKMASTER 1 (1945)

Centaurus-engined Buckmaster prototype *TJ714* on the Filton runway in 1945.

The Buckmaster was a dual-control trainer version of the type 164 Buckingham with a widened front fuselage to seat pilot and co-pilot side by side with the radio operator behind them.

Two prototypes and 100 production Buckmasters were built plus some conversions of Buckinghams. They were used as conversion trainers to familiarise pilots with the Brigand and Buckingham.

(Above)
BRISTOL TYPE 159 HEAVY BOMBER (1941)
The type 159 mock up in the Experimental Erecting Hall (Now Redux) on 14 January 1941. In the right foreground is the mock up of the proposed type 162 Beaumont.

In answer to Air Ministry spec. B1/39, Bristol submitted the design for an enlarged version of the Beaufort having four Bristol Hercules engines. A full size mock up was started but due to Filton's committment to the Blenheim, Beaufort and Beaufighter it was abandoned.

(Below)
BRISTOL 100 TON BOMBER (1943)
Official Wartime sketch of the proposed 100 ton Bomber.

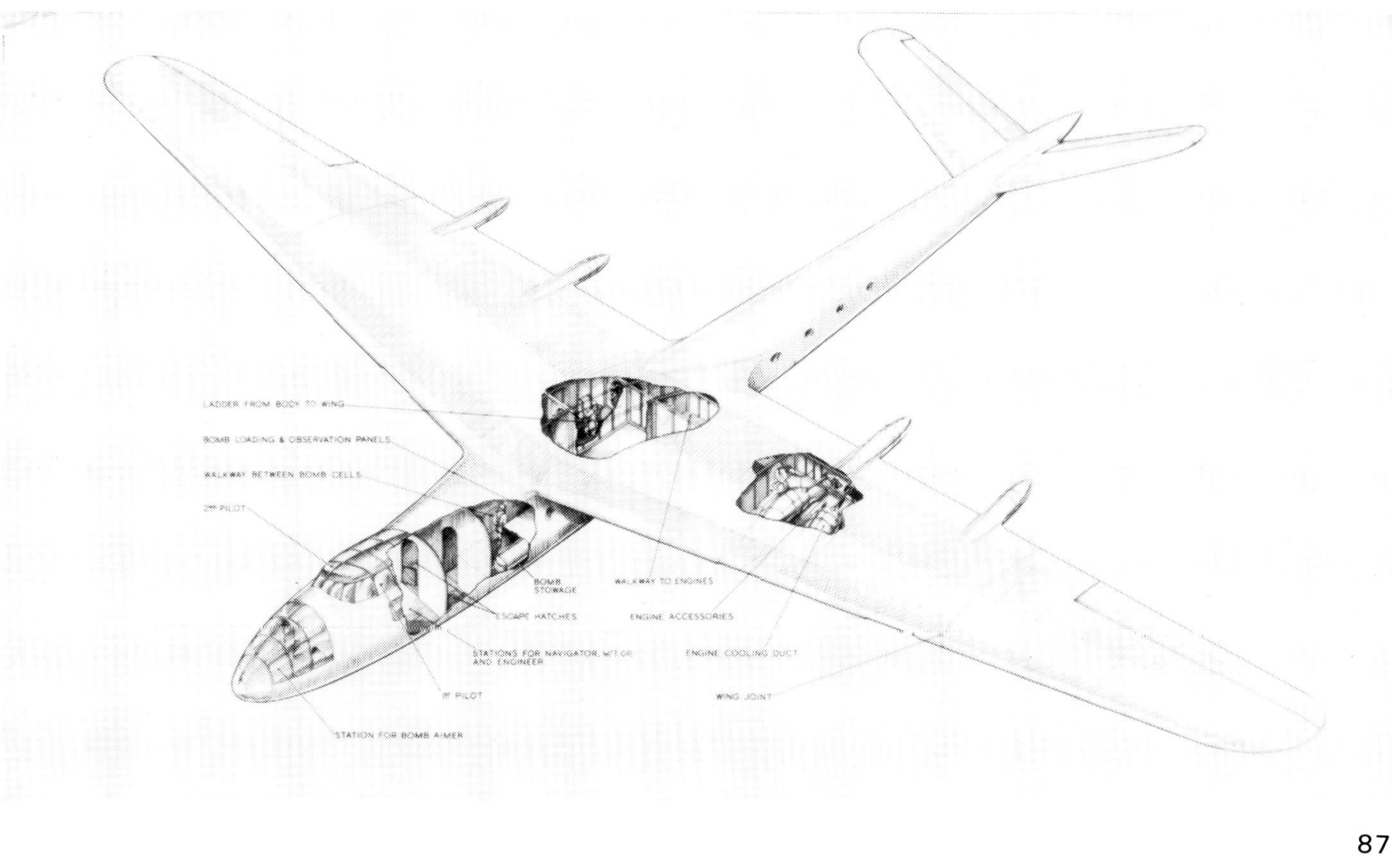

CHANGING FACE OF FILTON -3

The Works in 1939 just after being camouflage painted with new Filton House in the centre and Patchway engine works in the right distance.

Civilised Again

After the Battle of Britain, politicians and business people started to make provisional plans for the eventual return to civilian life. This may seem strange with hindsight because the War still had nearly five years to run but at that time nobody believed that the War could last more than another year or so.

Early in 1943 a committee was set up under the chairmanship of Lord Brabazon of Tara to consider the form that civil aircraft should take once hostilities had ceased. Five types of civil aircraft of various sizes and uses were recommended, the largest of which was a giant airliner to challenge the pre-War American lead and capable of flying an all weather London-New York service without intermediate refuelling stops.

Bristol was invited to undertake the design and manufacture of two prototypes provided that essential War work was not disrupted. The design followed generally the ideas put forward for the 100-ton bomber project and at least a dozen schemes were devised in the drawing office in Ivor House, Clifton. These covered high and low wing layouts, pusher and tractor propellers, 8 coupled *Centaurus* or 4 gas turbines, various diameter fuselages and even included a double-decker 50 berth 'flying hotel'. The design was finally settled as a mid wing monoplane of 230ft span, 170ft long and 50ft high powered by eight Bristol *Centaurus* 2650hp engines coupled in pairs to drive contra-rotating Rotol airscrews. Seating for up to 100 passengers was provided and the maximum take off weight was 290,000lbs (129 tons).

Drawings were issued in April 1945 and construction of the fuselage commenced in no.3 flight shed. To cater for the intended production a new 7½ acre assembly hangar was erected on the south side of the existing runway which itself had to be extended to twice its original length destroying the village of Charlton in the process.

After a year of ground testing, the Brabazon 1 mk.1 made its first flight on 4 September 1949 piloted by A.J. (Bill) Pegg, the Company's Chief Test Pilot. *G-AGPW* (originally Ministry of Supply *VX206*) was given its Certificate of Airworthiness on 14 June 1950.

(Below)
BRISTOL TYPE 167 BRABAZON I (1945)
The first Brabazon *G-AGPW* as few people saw it in 1950. From design studies for the 100 ton Bomber project, Filton was contracted to build an airliner of about 100 tons gross weight that was capable of flying non-stop from London to New York.

While *G-AGPW* was engaged on flight development, work started on a second machine *(VX343/G-AIML)* to be powered by Bristol *Proteus* turbo-prop engines and incorporating many structural refinements. However, following the newly elected Tory governments decision to cancel the project, it was never completed and both machines were cut up for scrap, in the hangar built for them, during October 1953.

The Bristol Brabazon 1 was the third largest piston engined aeroplane ever built and was the last aircraft to follow the principal of an ocean going liner with hotel services. Subsequent airliners adopted the concept long estalished on the railways and in coaching. It was an object lesson in how not, or why not, to build a large airframe but such is the risk taken in breaking new ground.

Freighter

Following the success during the 1939 War of the type 130 Bombay in Middle East operation, the type 170 was devised along similar lines but with a much larger fuselage and simplified wing and tail construction. Originally intended for use from jungle air-strips in the Far East, the maiden flight of the type 170 did not take place until 2 December 1945 — after the War had ended.

As there was a need for a robust freighter in civilian operation, and the Government was prepared to give financial assistance, the project continued in two civil forms. The type 170 Freighter was a utility machine with nose doors, although there were exceptions when the doors were fixed shut. The complimentary type 170 Wayfarer was a passenger version without nose doors but with interior trim and cabin heating. Wayfarers were much quicker to build than the Freighters with the nose doors so consequently early batches were built as Wayfarers. Sales of both versions were fairly brisk during 1946 and the 170 became the bread and butter of the Filton site in the immediate post war years.

A 'New Type 170' was introduced in 1947 which had a 10ft greater wing span, stronger airframe, more powerful Bristol *Hercules 672* engines and an all up weight of 40,000lb. The mk.21 was the basic freight only version while the mk.21E was for mixed passenger/freight traffic with the freight hold forward and a 16 seat passenger cabin aft, separated by a movable bulkhead. Cabin heating and other 'luxuries' made the 21E suitable for short haul flights of up to 900 miles. A military version of the 'New Type' was built for the Royal Pakistan Air Force and these mk.21M Freighters had parachute doors for supply dropping and windows in the lower portion of the nose doors. A mk.22A Wayfarer version of the New Type was offered but not built.

After two Freighters crashed during single-engine climb due to structural failure of the tail fin, a stronger dorsal fin was put into production resulting in the type 170 mk.31. Earlier machines were brought up to this standard at the next major overhaul. As well as the basic mk.31 Freighter, the mk.31E variant could carry cars and passengers. Military Freighters, mk.31M, were sold to the air forces of Canada, Pakistan, Burma, New Zealand and Iraq.

A special Freighter was built for Silver City Airways which had the nose extended by 5ft for the cross-Channel ferry service carrying 3 cars and 12 passengers. In addition to the 14 mk.32's sold to Silver City between 1953 and 1956, six were sold to Air Charter which also had some of its mk.31's converted to 'Superfreighters'.

Because of their very high utilisation most Bristol Freighters had a relatively short life in terms of years but of the 214 that were built, about six type 170's, including G-BISU, are still flying throughout the World.

(Below)
BRISTOL TYPE 170 FREIGHTER (1946)

The prototype freighter with fixed doors after being modified with a larger centrally mounted tail-plane but still with the round windows.

***G-AGPV* first flew on 2 December 1945 with Bristol Hercules 632 engines and in September 1946 was evaluated by the Air Ministry with the marking VR380.**

It was further modified with greater wing span, square side windows, various experimental radar installations and was flown until about 1963.

(Above)
BRISTOL TYPE 170 mk.21 (1947)
Freighter mk.21, G-AIME in Air Kruise livery circa 1947. Initially built as a mk.1, airframe no.12795 was delivered in 1947 to Suidair, registered ***ZE-BVI,*** after modification to mk.11A with round tipped wings of 108ft span. It later returned to the U.K., was given more powerful Hercules 672 engines to become Freighter mk.21 and was registered ***G-AIME.***

(Right Upper)
BRISTOL TYPE 170 mk.32 SUPERFREIGHTER (1955)
In its best known role as a cross Channel car ferry for Silver City Airways, mk.32 Superfreighter ***G-ANWN*** at work in the mid 1950's. ***G-ANWN*** was the last of six Superfreighters sold to Silver City in July 1956.

(Below)
BRISTOL TYPE 170 mk.31M (1954)
Burma Air Force Freighter mk.31M on 12 March 1954. After the loss of two aircraft, the type 170 was modified with a dorsal tail-fin and became mk.31. Eighty-eight mk.31 Freighters were built including 48 of the military version mk.31M and most were exported.

(Right Lower)
BRISTOL TYPE 170 mk.32 SUPERFREIGHTER (1953)
The first mk.32 which was originally registered ***G-AMLK.*** Introduced in 1953, the "Superfreighter" with 5ft longer nose could carry 3 cars plus 12 passengers or 2 cars plus 23 passengers. Eighteen mk. 32's with Bristol Hercules 734 engines were built at Filton from 1953 to 1957.

W
SILVER CITY

SILVER CITY

(Above)
BRISTOL TYPE 175 'BRITANNIA' 100 AIRLINER
The initial form of the 'Britannia', the series 100, would carry 90 tourist or 61 first class passengers.
The prototype, series 101, (*WB470*) first flew on 16 August 1952 and received the civil registration *G-ALBO.* A second -101 prototype, G-ALRX, was lost after ditching in the mud of the River Severn.
Fifteen production series 102 'Britannias' were sold to BOAC and, like the first two, were powered by Bristol Proteus 705 turboprop engines.

Britannia

The second recommendation of the Brabazon Committee, set up by the Wartime Government to suggest future civil aviation policy, was a medium range airliner for use on 'Empire routes'. At first it was proposed to meet this requirement by rebuilding existing Lockheed Constellations with Bristol *Centaurus* engines and to follow this with licenced production of Constellations.

This was unacceptable to the Government and was rejected in favour of a Bristol proposal for a type 175 low wing passenger monoplane using *Centaurus* piston engines.

At that time, 1946-47, the new high compression Bristol propeller turbine engine which was to be the successor fo the Bristol *Theseus* was still in the design stage.

The Bristol *Theseus* propeller gas turbine engine, the first gas turbine to be built at Bristol Engines, was designed from 1941 onwards. Ministerial permission was granted in 1944 for detailed design and manufacture and the *Theseus* first ran 'on the bench' in July 1945 becoming in December 1946 the first propeller turbine in the World to pass a type test. It was flight tested in a Lincoln bomber during 1947. Its high compression descendant became the Bristol *Proteus* free turbine engine.

Three prototypes of the type 175 transport were ordered by the Ministry of Supply in July 1948. All were to be built with Bristol *Centaurus* piston engines but the later two were to be suitable for conversion to take the new *Proteus* turbine engine when it became available for flight. Prototypes 1 and 2 were to be bare airframes but the third was to be furnished to airline standard.

The *Proteus* made such good progress that it was decided to drop the interim *Centaurus* engined design and go for *Proteus* power from the outset. The programme for the prototypes was rearranged so that the two airframes suitable for *Proteus* engines became flying prototypes while the initial *Centaurus* engined airframe became a functional mock-up for ground testing.

First of the flying prototypes, *G-ALBO,* took to the air on 16 August 1952 in the hands of Bill Pegg and was then exhibited at Farnborough. *G-ALRX,* the second Britannia, achieved first flight on 23 December 1953 but its life was short because it was ditched in the mud of the River Severn on 4 February 1954 after an engine fire. It was subsequently written off but survived for many years as an instructional airframe, albeit in parts, in the Bristol Engines training school.

Fifteen production medium range Britannias, *G-ANBA* to *G-ANBO,* were built for BOAC with *G-ANBA* flying on 5 September 1954 after which it was used for development flying for a time. Deliveries to BOAC commenced on 30 December 1955. The Britannia was late entering airline service, actually starting on 1 February 1957 on the Johannesburg run, because during route proving trials over Africa in 1956 problems with engine 'flame out' had been experienced. This was tracked down to ice forming in the air intake 'S'-ducts to the engines and delays were inevitable while a cure was being affected. BOAC's order was completed and delivered by August 1957.

A freighter version (series 200) of the Britannia was proposed in 1952 which had a 10ft-3in longer fuselage to facilitate the adding of a side loading cargo door ahead of the propellers. It was not built because BOAC could not obtain I.A.T.A. clearance for an all freight operation but consideration was then given to alternative uses for a longer Britannia. Included in the proposed range were cargo/ passenger (series 250), medium range passenger (series 300) and long range passenger (series 300LR) versions.

BOAC converted its option for another ten 'short' Britannia 100 series to an order for ten series 300 and 300LR. This order was later reduced to eight and finally cancelled in favour of a new long range Britannia.

Of the eight aircraft laid down for BOAC, *G-ANCA* to *G-ANCH,* the prototype *G-ANCA* which first flew on 31 July 1955 was purchased by the Ministry of Supply but crashed at Downend on 6 November 1957. A World sales tour resulted in sales of the remaining seven. *G-ANCB/G-ANCC* with medium range tanks were sold to Aeronauves de Mexico registered *XA-MEC/XA-MED.*

The five aircraft with long range capacity were built on the secondary production line set up by Bristol at Short Brothers and Harland in Belfast. *G-ANCD* was leased to Air Charter Limited in 1959 and bought by it in 1961 after being on lease for a while to E1 A1 and joined *G-ANCE.* Transcontinental of the Argentine bought ex *G-ANCF/G-ANCG* in 1959 and registered them *LV-GJB/LV-GJC* while the last one, *G-ANCH,* was sold to Ghana Airways as *9G-AAG* as late as 1960. Most were modified internally before delivery.

The new long range Britannia was designated series 310 and had a stronger fuselage effected by increasing the thickness of the aluminium skin. *G-AOVA,* the first -310 flew on 31 December 1956 and was used for development until sold to Ghana Airways. BOAC bought 18 of the series 310 (variant-312) and put them on the London-New York service commencing in November 1957.

It is ironic that what started life as a 'Medium Range Empire' airliner should find its greatest success on long haul flights across the Atlantic and on trans-continental work. El Al, in fact, used three of its -313's on a non-stop service from New York to Tel Aviv — distance of 6,100 miles. Thirty five of the series 310 variants were sold to home and overseas operators including one leased third hand to Czechoslovakia.

Of the series 250 cargo/passenger version of the Britannia, three -252's were bought by the Ministry of Supply and had wooden cabin floors. These were followed by twenty -253's with metal floors for RAF Transport Command. Five of the -253's (XM498; XM517-XM520) were built at Filton but the remaining 15 and the -252's were erected at Shorts in Belfast. All 23 were delivered in 1959/60 and became the last Britannias in service for when the RAF retired them in 1976 some were certified for civilian use.

The Britannia 320 series, originally offered in 1956, was an 'Americanised' version of the long range 310 but having medium range fuel tanks, air stairs, larger

(Below)
BRISTOL TYPE 175 BRITANNIA 102 (1955)
G-ANBA **was the first airline Britannia and was one of fifteen sold to BOAC up to 1957.**

panoramic windows and seats for up to 133 passengers. Four Britannia -318's were built to 320 standard in 1959 and sold to Cubana (*CU-T668* to *CU-T671*). Two -324's were built for stock and were leased to Canadian Pacific Airlines from 1959 to 1961 after which they were sold to British Eagle Airways (*G-ARKA/G-ARKB*). *G-ARKB,* constructors number 13517, was the last Britannia to be built in 1959 by which time the type 175, like all other turbo-prop airliners, was being rapidly overtaken both literally and figuratively on long distance services by the pure jets such as the de Havilland Comet 4 and Boeing 707.

(Right Upper)
BRISTOL TYPE 175 'BRITANNIA' 300 AIRLINER.
The next development of the Britannia, collectively known as the series 300, had the fuselage lengthened by 10'-3'' to provide accommodation for 101 tourist passengers but with a slightly reduced range. Proteus 755 engines were used.
Transcontinental's series 308 Britannia with temporary registration *LV-PPJ* later *G-ANCF* and was built in Belfast by Short Brothers and Harland Limited, a Bristol subsidiary. Other customers included Ghana and Mexico.

(Right Centre)
BRISTOL TYPE 175 BRITANNIA 320 AIRLINER.
The series 320 standard was a medium range version of the long fuselage Britannia and could carry 133 people for up to 3,500 miles.
Cunard Eagle's series 324(G-ARKA) was originally registered *CF-CPD* and was one of two machines originally leased to Canadian Pacific Airlines.

(Below)
BRISTOL TYPE 175 BRITANNIA 310 AIRLINER
***G-AOVB* was the first of 19 series 312 Britannias sold to BOAC and was a long range version suitable for trans-Atlantic flights.**
Aircraft in this group (series 311 to 318) had the fuselage 10'-3'' longer than the original series 100 and could carry 60 first class or 90 tourist passengers for almost 5,000 miles. Similar Britannias were sold to E1 A1 Israel Airlines, Canadian Pacific and Cubana.

(Right Lower)
BRISTOL TYPE 175 BRITANNIA 250
***XN392* of RAF Support Command (formerly Transport Command) was originally *G-APPE* built in Belfast for the Ministry of Supply and was officially series 252 (Coastal mk.2).**
A cargo-passenger version with heavy duty floor stressed to carry heavy loads in the forward section of the fuselage it had a movable bulkhead to separate the cargo and passenger areas. (*Crown Copyright*).

TRANSCONTINENTAL
LV-PPJ

CUNARD EAGLE AIRWAYS

392
ROYAL AIR FORCE AIR SUPPORT COMMAND

Canadair

In March 1954 Canadair Limited took out a licence with the Bristol Aeroplane Company for the production of Britannia variants in Montreal, Canada.

For maritime reconnaissance duties by the Royal Canadian Air Force, Canadair built the CL-28 Argus transport having an unpressurised and unfurnished Britannia-type airframe. Powered by four Wright *Turbo-Compound* piston engines with low fuel consumption it could stay airborne on patrol for up to 24 hours. The Argus entered service in September 1957 and 33 had been delivered before production ceased in 1960.

CL-44-6, Yukon, the second Canadair transport was based on the Britannia 253 with longer fuselage and four Rolls Royce *Tyne* turbo prop engines. Twelve Yukons with side loading freight doors were sold to the RCAF which designated them CC106.

Twenty-eight CL-44D-4 freighters followed which had an unusual hinged rear fuselage which could be swung open for the rear loading of freight into the body of the aircraft. First flown in November 1960 they were also sold to private operators with typically North American names like Seaboard World Airlines, The Flying Tiger Line and Slick Airways. Production of this last Canadair 'Bristol' aircraft continued until 1964, long after Britannia production had finished at Filton, and gave the Filton purse a useful boost when it was most needed.

Britannic

Several other Bristol projects deserve mention here for although they did not come to fruition they had some influence on subsequent events. They used Freighter or Britannia ideas where appropriate for a four engined transport suitable for the needs of the RAF.

The first project, type 179 of 1951, was a 4-*Hercules* engined high wing transport as a replacement for the type 170. At first it was proposed to use twin tail booms but later changed to a conventional rear fuselage having an upswept under surface incorporating a power operated loading ramp. A similar later design in 1955 was for a mid wing rear loading transport, type 195, using the wing and 4 Bristol *Proteus* turbo-props as used in the Britannia.

The short SC5 transport announced in February 1959, at first suggested to be named Britannic but built as the Belfast, was very similar to the proposed type 179B fuselage and used a Filton designed Britannia type wing mounted high on the fuselage. Other Britannia parts were used where possible to reduce cost. The Belfast had four Rolls-Royce *Tyne* turboprop engines and ten were built in Northern Ireland by Short Brothers and Harland, an associate of the Bristol Aeroplane Company, using wings built at Filton. It first flew in 1962 and entered service with no.10 squadron RAF in 1966. The decision to erect the Belfast in Belfast was taken by the Government which while pressing English 'plane makers to merge, considered Northern Ireland as a special case.

As early as 1953 time was taken to consider the design of a replacement for the Britannia emerging as the type 187 long range transport. It was to have a "double bubble" (figure 8 section fuselage) and four of the new Bristol *Orion* turbo prop engines. The *Orion*

(Below)
CANADAIR CL-28 ARGUS (1957)
Argus, serial no.*VN710* in service with 405 squadron, Royal Canadian Air Force.
The Argus was based on a maritime reconnaissance version of the Britannia and was built under licence in Montreal, Canada. Thirty-three CL-28's with Wright piston engines were sold to the RCAF between 1957 and 1960.

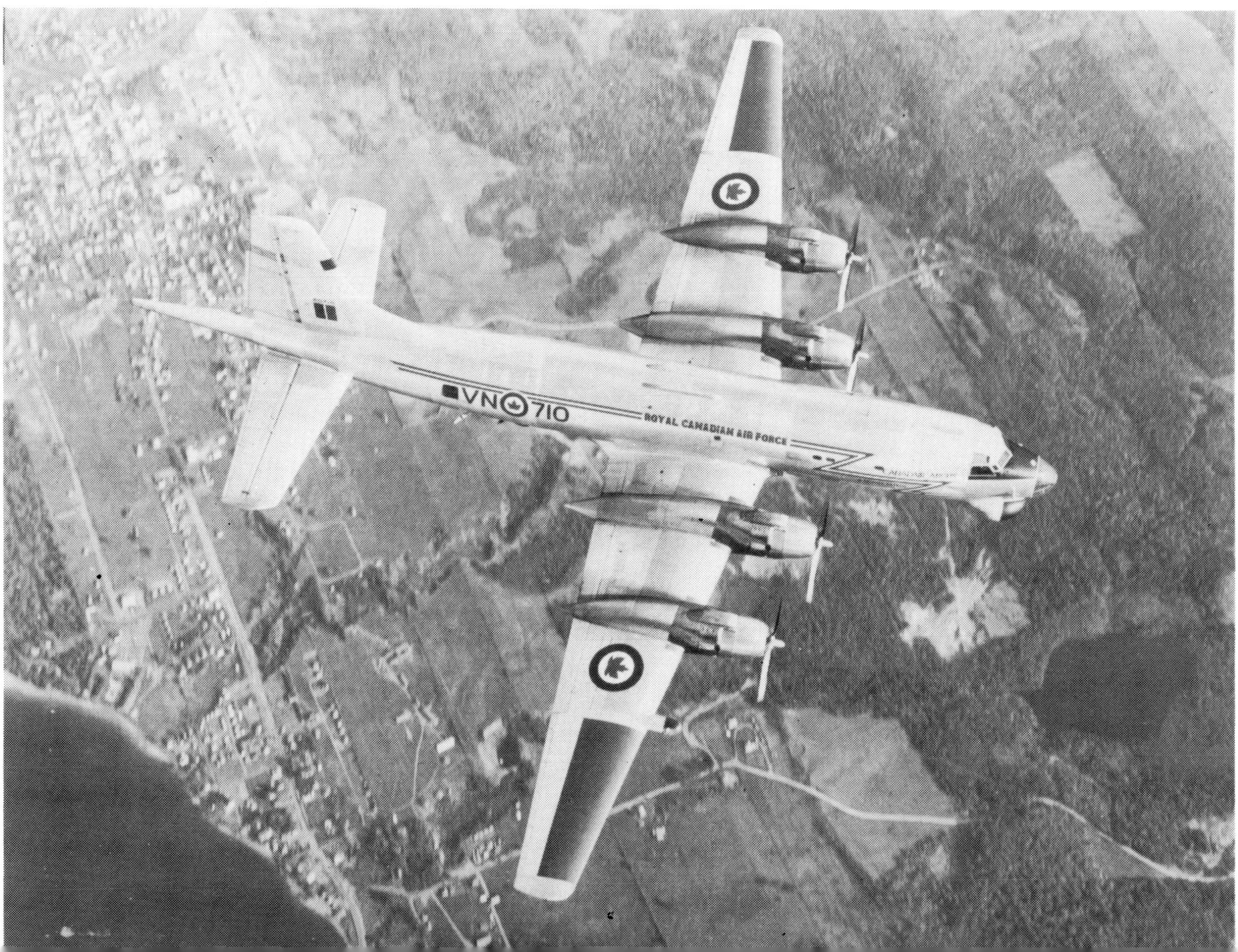

(Above)
SHORT SC5 BELFAST (1960)
Belfast *no.364* at the 1964 Farnborough Air Show. Originally intended to be named Britannic, the Belfast was based on Filton ideas but for political reasons was built by Short Brothers & Harland in Northern Ireland. The fuselage was similar to the proposed Bristol type 179B and it used a Britannia-derived wing built at Filton. (*Dick Wood*).

(Below)
BRISTOL-FERRANTI BLOODHOUND MISSILE (1957)
Developed under the code name Red Duster during the early 1950's it made the first ever direct hit by a British surface to air missile when it intercepted a Firefly target aircraft over Cardigan Bay in 1957.
As the Bloodhound, it entered service with the RAF at North Coates, Lincolnshire in 1957. It used 4 solid fuel jetisonable boosters for take off and 2 Bristol *Thor* ramjets for the main propulsion to the target.

was flight tested but its development was later curtailed by the Tory Government in favour of the Rolls Royce *Tyne* and with it went the hopes for the type 187. Plans were also in the pipeline to re-engine the existing Britannias with the *Orion* but met with structural problems.

A maritime reconnaissance version of the Britannia was schemed in 1955 along similar lines to the Canadair Argus with 4- Napier *Nomad* engines. Airframe sequence number 13209 was allocated to it but it did not progress.

As a successor to the Freighter, the type 216 was proposed in 1959 for Silver City Airways to replace its mk.32 'Superfreighters' on the cross-Channel ferry link.

Bristol Aircraft Limited

During the production life of the Britannia a further reorganisation of the Company had occurred in January 1956 when three subsidiary companies were formed — Bristol Aircraft Limited, Bristol Aero-Engines Limited and Bristol Cars — each wholly owned by the Bristol Aeroplane Company.

Seven overseas subsidiary companies were also formed, mainly as servicing and sales outlets, in Canada, Australia, New Zealand and Mexico. Short Brothers and Harland, Rotol (jointly owned by Rolls Royce) and British Messier were the most important of the six associated companies; the others being in France, Spain and Australia.

To service the smaller locations, forty overseas representatives, agents and concessionaires were appointed thus bringing Bristol products to all five continents.

Beside fixed wing aircraft Bristol had expanded its interests to cover helicopters and guided weapons and these became divisions of Bristol Aircraft Limited.

(Above)
BRISTOL TYPE 176 (1948)
Wooden model of proposed swept wing research aircraft.
The type 176 was to be flying scale model for high speed research in connection with the proposed type 172 High Speed Long Range Bomber (1946). The bomber specification was eventually met by the Vickers Valiant, Avro Vulcan and Handley Page Victor.

(Below)
BRISTOL TYPE 182R RED RAPIER (1953)
Early cruise missile — retrievable prototype of a 600mph bomber at Filton in July 1953.
Under the code name Red Rapier, a pilotless, radio-controlled expendable bomber, type 182, was devised at Filton. It was to be made of the Durestos material used for drop tanks and a retrievable metal prototype, type 182R, was built using a 'throw away' Bristol jet engine.
The project was cancelled but the engine was developed and became the Bristol *Orpheus* turbojet which powered the Folland Gnat and other aircraft at home and overseas.

Helicopters

The idea of a revolving wing aircraft dates back at least to the time of Leonardo da Vinci but the first practical design was the Autogiro produced by Juan de la Cierva in 1923. Igor Sikorsky, an American of Russian descent, was the first to produce a series of helicopters and had given the USA the lead in that field through his inventions.

Bristol's involvement in helicopters started after the 1939 War and was based on the work of Austrian Raoul Hafner. With Ministry of Supply funding, a design team headed by Hafner was set-up at Filton. Two prototypes of a single rotor type 171 helicopter using a Pratt and Whitney *Wasp Junior* engine were constructed and flown in 1947/48. These were followed by a prototype Sycamore type 171 mk.2 with an Alvis Leonides engine in September 1949.

Fifteen production 171 mk.3 were erected between 1950 and 1954 and all but a demonstrator, *G-ALSX,* were sold to the M.o.S. Variants of 171 mk.3 were supplied to the individual requirements of British European Airways, the RAF and the Australian Navy.

The Sycamore mk.4 introduced in 1953 was an attempt to produce a standard helicopter that could be adapted to particular needs and the prototype, *G-AMWI,* flew in May. By 1959 sales of the Sycamore mk.4 had reached 151 plus two airframes built as spares and included sales to Germany, Australia, Belgium as well as the RAF. A sycamore is now preserved in Bristol Industrial Museum.

The type 173 twin rotor helicopter was a research and development aircraft designed primarily to gain knowledge of twin engined tandem rotor configurations. Five prototypes were ordered by the Ministry of Supply and the first, *G-ALBN,* was flown on 3 January 1952. It was joined in trials by *G-AMJI* in 1953 but the third type 173 was delayed until 1956 and the last two were never flown.

Derived from the type 173, the type 192 with Napier *Gazelle* turbo-shaft engines was designed for troop or freight carrying, ambulance duties and search and reescue work. By the time that the prototype *(XG447)* flew on 5 July 1958, helicopter construction had been transferred to Old Mixon, Weston-Super-Mare. The move had actually started in March 1955. Belvedere was the name adopted for the type 192 and 26 were built for the RAF mostly after the Helicopter Division had become a part of Westland Aircraft Limited in February 1960 on the formation of the British Aircraft Corporation.

The type 188 supersonic research aircraft was the last true Bristol aeroplane to be built and its purpose was to explore the effects of kinetic heating of the airframe at speeds up to three times the speed of sound (mach.3 or 1,980 mph at 36000 ft). Two flying examples (*XF923* and *XF926*) powered by two D.H. *Gyron Junior* engines were built plus a structural test airframe. The first one flew on 14 April 1962, nine years after it had been conceived. Extensive use was made of stainless steel requiring special welding techniques to be developed. It was originally part of a programme to develop future supersonic military aircraft and later, as a sideline, to help prove that the mach.2 S.S.T. airframe could be made from conventional aluminium alloys. Due to high fuel consumption they totalled only about 25 hours in the air before being retired from flying duties in 1964. One type 188 is now preserved.

(Left)
BRISTOL DROP TANKS (1959)
Bristol 100 gallon drop tank no B1/66126/E made at Filton in June 1961 posed in front of an F86 Sabre with similar tanks.

The plastics division of Bristol Aircraft Limited developed an expendable drop tank made from Durestos, a non strategic asbestos phenolic material, which was patented in 1959 (no. 781, 924).

Standard sizes of 50, 100, 150, 200, 300 and 500 gal capacity were produced as well as specials for individual aircraft. Each tank was made, by hot gluing, in three sections which could be stored nested together and be assembled in the field by 2 or 3 men with a screwdriver.

(Below)
BRISTOL TYPE 188 (1962)
***XF923,* the first of three type 188 supersonic research aircraft, during one of its nineteen subsonic flights. The type 188 was the last new design to carry the Bristol name.**

Design commenced in 1953 but due to difficulties in fabricating the stainless steel airframe *XF923* did not fly until 1962 in British Aircraft Corporation days. The potential of the type 188 technology has yet to be exploited to full advantage.

"Bristol"
HOUSING
MODERN EFFICIENCY IN THE HOME
THE ALUMINIUM HOUSE
THE BRISTOL AEROPLANE COMPANY (HOUSING) LTD OLDMIXON, WESTON-SUPER-MARE
WORK BENCH
COOKER
WASH BOILER
SINK
REFRIGERATOR
BROOMS

OHY 401

(Left Upper)
BRISTOL PREFABRICATED HOUSE (1945)
Demonstration unit on its trailer at Old Mixon in the 1940's. As the last Beaufighter rolled down the production line at the Old Mixon shadow factory in 1945 it was followed by the first of over 1,000 A.I.R.O.H. 'prefabs'.
Besides houses and hospitals, schools, municipal buildings and coal pit wash houses were also built. The Bristol prefab first flew in 1945 along the A370.

(Left Lower)
BRISTOL 401 (1949)
When aircraft work was difficult to obtain after the Second War, Bristol diversified into other work including the pretigious range of two litre sports cars. Later Bristol cars didn't quite have the same beauty as the 401.

(Above)
BRISTOL 405 (1955)

Non-Aircraft Products

(Below)
Prototype light alloy freight container built at Filton in 1959.

(Above Left)
BRISTOL TYPE 171 SYCAMORE (1953)
Prototype Sycamore mk.4 helicopter *G-AMWI* during a civil defence exercise near Bristol Cars (in background) and adjacent to the present "Pyramids."
Type 171 mk.4 was the Company demonstrator and the first Bristol helicopter to have right hand drive as American practise.

(Above)
BRISTOL SYCAMOR
Sycamore *XD654*
in the smoke or HM

YPE 171 mk.51 (1953)
:rials with the Australian Navy framed
/engeance in January 1953.

(Above Right)
BRISTOL BELVEDERE TYPE 192 (1958)
Tandem rotor helicopter *XG448* was the second of 26 type 192's built between 1958 and 1962.

A development of the type 173, the Belvedere was produced especially for the RAF and used two Napier Gazelle turbo-shaft engines. All Belvederes were assembled at Weston and the last ones were made after the transfer of the Bristol Helicopter Division to Westland's in 1960.

(Left)
BRISTOL TYPE 173 mk.2 ROTOCOACH (1953)
The second type 173 twin rotor helicopter (*G-AMJI*) built at Filton in 1953 and shown at the Farnborough Air Show in that year.

Powered by two Alvis Leonides Major piston engines the rotor gearboxes were linked by a longitudinal shaft so that it could fly on one engine in an emergency. After a few flights the stub wings were replaced by a dihedral tailplane for Admiralty trials as a carrier based helicopter. It carried the M.o.S. serial *XH379* in that form.

British Aircraft Corporation

At the end of World War 2 there were 27 airframe manufacturers and 8 aero-engine makers in the U.K., although some of these did have a corporate link up. Bristol, Blackburn and de Havilland made airframes and engines so the picture was not quite as diverse as it might seem at first glance.

Inevitably there was some duplication of effort which, when combined with the increasing complexity and expense of new projects, was not in the best interest of the Country in general. The few projects that were available in the 1950's were not sufficient to sustain all of these organisations.

In addition, the 1957 Defence White Paper dealt a severe blow to the British aircraft industry by declaring that the defence of Britain was to be by nuclear weapons and that their delivery was to be by unmanned rockets instead of piloted aeroplanes. The philosophy behind this decision was based almost entirely on cost and the need to reduce defence expenditure.

To further compound the problem it became official policy to reshape the British aircraft industry by force through the selective placing of orders. As Whitehall was the principal customer for military aircraft and a prime source of revenue for the aircraft makers it was not difficult, or indeed unreasonable, for the Government to apply whatever conditions it thought to be appropriate.

Government pressure was first evident in the procurement of a supersonic tactical strike and reconnaissance aircraft to operational requirement OR339 to succeed the English Electric Canberra bomber. Bristol for its part had proposed the type 204 with two Bristol *Olympus* engines in 1957 and other firms had put forward ideas.

The order was, however, given to Vickers Armstrongs and English Electric in 1959 with the proviso that there was to be close cooperation between the two companies. Bristol Engine Division was given an order for *Olympus* engines to power the new TSR2, which was the only military aircraft contract then on offer by the Ministry, provided that it merged with Armstrong Siddeley Motors.

New work on the civil aircraft side was equally as hard to obtain with the main requirement being the BEA medium range transport for which the Bristol type 200 was a prime contender.

As a consequence of the Tory Governments policy enforced by Duncan Sandys, the British Aircraft Corporation was formed on 1 July 1960 by the merging of the interests of English Electric, Vickers and Bristol Aeroplane in the ratio of 40:40:20 with Bristol as the poor relation. This was a complex arrangement whereby each of the three companies kept its corporate identity yet were combined to work on new projects in line with the Whitehall edict.

(Below)
BRISTOL TYPE 221.
The last aircraft to fly with a Bristol designation was not entirely a Bristol design. The 221 was originally the famous Fairey *Delta 2* in which Peter Twiss achieved a record speed of 1,132 mph on 10 March 1956 and was the first aircraft in the World to exceed 1000 mph.
It was an obvious choice for an experimental aircraft for testing the Ogee wing proposed for the mach 2 supersonic transport project. It first flew on 1 May 1964 and was used extensively in the early stages of the Concorde programme.

The early 'sixties were bad years because none of the three constituent companies could look foward to sufficient support for its new projects and had to rely on existing work to survive. Bristol was particularly badly placed and there was little work in the Filton 'shops. Britannia construction was quickly becoming a thing of the past, the order for the BEA transport had gone to the Hawker Siddeley Trident and the type 188 research aircraft only kept a small proportion of the Works occupied. Some non-aircraft work had been undertaken in 1959 including a prototype semi-trailer with aluminium alloy van body.

Without new work the Filton airframe site was in grave danger but this was averted to some degree by the transfer of work on the Lightning mk.IV from English Electric at Warton and VC10 work from Weybridge. Later, the conversion of the Fairey FD2 to ogee wing, which had originally been awarded to Hunting Aircraft, was transferred to Filton and became the Bristol type 221.

The first BAC aeroplane was the One-Eleven largely based on the Hunting H107 — Hunting Aircraft having joined BAC in 1961. The proposed H107 was enlarged and the Bristol Siddeley *BS75* engines replaced by Rolls Royce *RB163 Spey* turbojets.

Production of the BAC One Eleven twin jet airliner commenced in 1961 and was shared by Hurn (final assembly), Luton, Weybridge and Filton (tail and fin).

First flown in the autumn of 1963, over 220 One Elevens were sold with two thirds being for export and, although not a massive amount of work was involved at Filton, the One Eleven was useful during the lean years before Concorde.

Most people outside the aircraft industry could be forgiven for assuming that Concorde was the only aircraft built by BAC. It was certainly the most famous and undoubtedly gave Filton and the other BAC sites a vast amount of work to do.

(Above)

The series 500 was the largest of the BAC One-Eleven family of short/medium range twin jet airliners.

(Left)

BAC ONE ELEVEN (1963)

Construction of One Eleven tail assembly for Rumania in the Redux Shop.

Filton built the empennage of the early batches of One Elevens before the advent of Concorde and again, for the ROMBAC contract, in the late 1970's. 237 units were delivered to Hurn between 1962 and 1981.

(Below)

BAC TSR2 (1960)

Bristol had to yield to Government pressure to get the order for the Olympus engines for the TSR2 and by merging the Engine Division with Armstrong Siddeley Motors ceased to be an independent aero engine manufacturer.

The idea of a supersonic transport was based on work done on delta wings at Farnborough and, after the Supersonic Transport Committee reported in 1959 that the project was possible, design study contracts were awarded to Bristol and Hawker Siddeley.

Bristol proposed the type 198 using six *Olympus* turbojet engines grouped together at first above the wing but later in two nacelles beneath the wings. A triple nacelle version was also considered as were aluminium and, alternatively, steel airframes. Complementary to these schemes was the type 213 designed to fly at speeds up to mach 3. It was eventually decided to use a light alloy airframe and to restrict the speed to mach.2.2 (1,400 mph) because this would be the least complicated and therefore have less chance of being cancelled during construction. This long range version type 223 was submitted in 1961.

One of the conditions imposed by the Government on the embryo SST project was that collaboration be sought with another country in order to reduce the cost to the U.K. Across the Pond, the USA was proceeding with a mach 3 steel and titanium airframe and was not interested in the 223. Sud Aviation in France had a proposal on the drawing board for a medium range SST known as the Super Caravelle and the subsequent association with the French happened simply because there was no other suitable partner available.

The conflict between the two partners over the choice of long or medium range delayed the project and exacerbated the problems of difference of national personality. Long range eventually won the day but not before two medium range prototypes had been built. — 001 *(F-WTSS)* attaining first flight on 2 March 1969 and 002 *(G-BSST)* on 9 April 1969.

Two pre-production aircraft, 01 and 02, followed which were longer than the prototypes and had other refinements in the light of operational, manufacturing and research experience. Filton-built 01 became airborne on 17 December 1971 and 02 at Toulouse on 10 January 1972.

Preparations were made for the production of 22 Concordes to be finally assembled at Filton and Toulouse using parts and sub-assemblies from Preston, Filton, Weybridge and Sud factories. In addition, the services of a small army of sub contractors and equipment suppliers was enlisted.

There was not any duplication of effort — a single design office or manufacturer being responsible for a particular part of the aircraft structure that was used on both French and British Concordes.

In the heyday of Concorde there were 74 orders and options and Filton seemed set for plenty of work for many years to come but it didn't quite work out that way.

Despite the efforts of environmentalists in America and the anti Concorde lobby at home, Concorde went into airline service on 21 January 1976 and proved itself to be a winner, with the passengers if not with the accountants. Of the twenty Concordes that have flown only fourteen are to airline standard and only British Airways has really made an effort to get the best out of the colossal investment.

As Concorde approaches its tenth year in revenue service the scheduled routes show good profitability and the charter side is doing very well. Many people still consider a trip in Concorde to be the flight of a lifetime and it is not difficult to fully book an excursion.

Whatever ones personal viewpoint, the Concorde is undoubtedly the most advanced civil aircraft in the World and is unlikely to be beaten in this century.

(Below)
BRISTOL TYPE 223.S.S.T. (1961)
Sketch of proposed type 223 Super-Sonic Transport with light alloy airframe and Bristol Olympus turbojet engines.
After various design schemes for a S.S.T. involving aluminium and steel airframes, Bristol evolved the type 223 with ogival wing and four Olympus. This proposal for a mach 2.2 long range S.S.T. dated September 1961 formed at least half of the Anglo-French Concorde — the other half being the medium-range Sud Aviation Super Caravelle.

(Right Upper)
BAC CONCORDE 202.
***G-BBDG,* the second pre-production Concorde in British Airways livery during a test flight.**
After the two prototypes and two pre-production Concordes had flown, eight production Concordes were assembled at Filton for British Airways as well as eight similar aircraft assembled by Aerospatiale at Tolouse for Air France.

(Right Lower)
Concorde assembly at Filton with *G-BOAA* top left and *G-BOAE* top right of the picture.

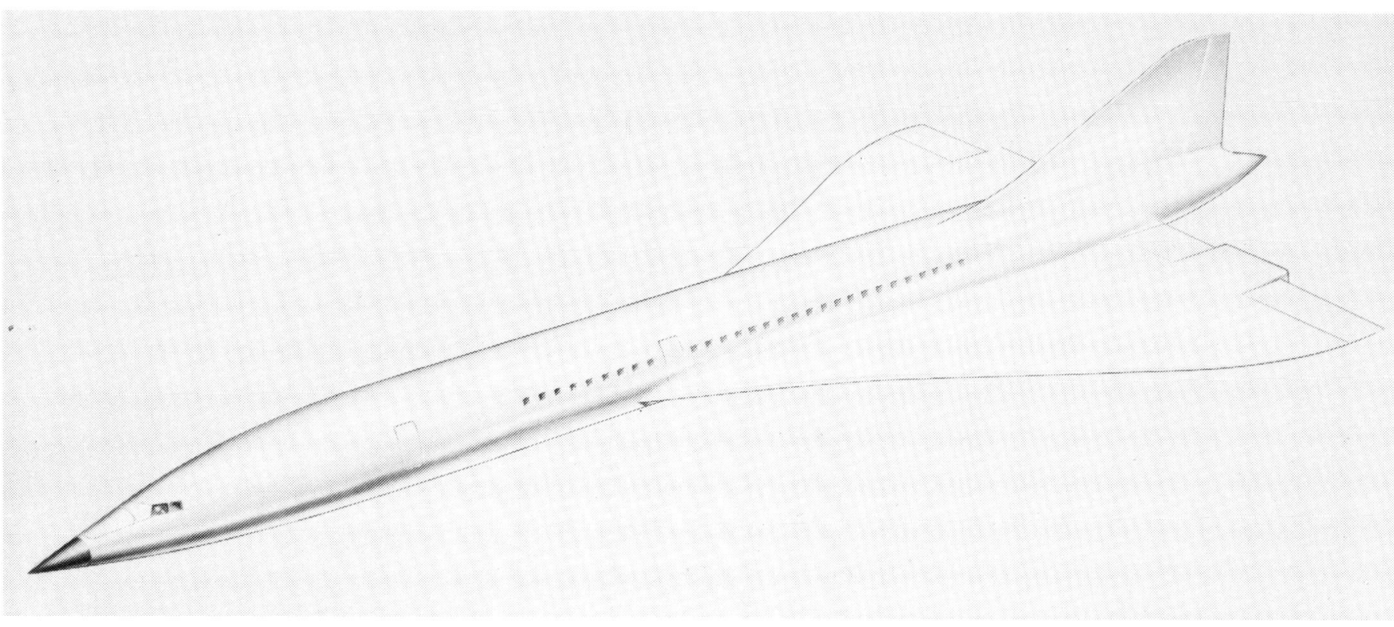

G-BBDG

British airways
NO SMOKING

Bristol Aerospace

Under the provisions of "The Aircraft and Shipbuilding Industries Act 1977", a nationalised corporation — British Aerospace — was established. On 29 April 1977 the issued share capital of The British Aircraft Corporation, Hawker-Siddeley Aircraft, Hawker-Siddeley Dynamics and Scottish Aviation was vested in the new corporation which then acquired the assets and businesses of these companies on 1 January 1978. Public ownership was short-lived, however, for it became a public limited company — British Aerospace PLC. — on 1 January 1981.

The Aircraft Group of British Aerospace has united some of the most famous names in British aviation; Avro (Manchester), Blackburn (Brough), Bristol (Filton), de Havilland (Hatfield and Chester), English Electric (Preston and Warton), Folland (Hamble), Sopwith/Hawker (Kingston) and Vickers (Weybridge). Filton is also associated with Stevenage and Hatfield as part of the Dynamics Group.

As far as Filton is concerned, BAe could stand for Bits of Aeroplanes because, apart from the diminutive Stabileye, Bristol has not assembled a complete aircraft since the last Concorde was delivered in June 1980.

When aircraft orders have been scarce in the past, the various Boards of Directors have always been able to secure a healthy profit from Filton. Adapting the Works to suit changing patterns of available work has become an art in itself and a way of life after 75 years of practice.

The **Tornado** multi role combat aircraft is British Aerospace's most important military project and is built by a consortium formed in 1970 and comprising British Aerospace (at that time BAC), Messersmitt-Bolkow-Blohm and Aeritalia. Production of the Tornado supersonic swing-wing aircraft commenced in 1976 and the

(Above)
PANAVIA TORNADO.
Filton has contributed to the design of the multi-national MRCA and makes the wing slat and flap rails in addition to parts of the cockpit.

(Below)
Turbo-Union RB199 engine removed from Tornado XZ630 in 1982.
The RB199 trubofan for the Tornado all weather multirole combat aircraft forms about one third of the current production of the Bristol Engine Division of Rolls Royce at Patchway. (*Rolls Royce*).

(Above)
BAe 146.
The fuselage of the BAe 146 static strength test specimen being manoeuvred into the water tank at Filton late in 1980.
After the assembly of the tailplane and wings, the flying surfaces were operated by jacks to simulate landing and take-off. The airframe was tested to destruction in more cycles than any one aircraft will see in service.

(Inset)
BAE 146.
G-SSHH the first HS146 feeder jet airliner originally devised by Hawker Siddeley and finally assembled at BAe Hatfield for which Bristol supplies the centre fuselage.

(Below)
BAe 146.
The third BAe 146 centre fuselage to be built at Filton being prepared for its journey by road to Hatfield in February 1981.

first 75 aircraft had been delivered in 1980. BAe as a whole is responsible for the manufacture of the forward and rear sections of the fuselage, fin and tail for all Tornado's and final assembly of aircraft to be delivered to the RAF. Filton's contribution has included the machining of components for the cockpit, taileron skins, slat rails and flap rails. Production of the Tornado will gradually diminish until 1988 by which time a total of over 809 aircraft will have been delivered to the RAF, Luftwaffe or Italian Air Force.

When Concorde production finished, the "Brab Hangar" now raised in status to the "Aircraft Assembly Hall" was occupied by nine interlopers from Weybridge. These ex-airline **Vickers VC10's** have been converted to Air to Air Refuelling Tankers for the RAF to supplement the fleet of Handley Page Victors already in service.

The Hawker-Siddeley HS146 was originally conceived in the late 'sixties, was then suspended but revived as the **BAe 146** in 1978. First deliveries of the BAe 146, which is assembled at Hatfield, were made in 1982. It was responsible for the revival of the Filton sub-assembly shops from the doldrums which followed the run down of Concorde.

Filton builds the centre fuselage incorporating the wing box as its contribution but has also been responsible for fatigue testing of the static test airframe for Certification of the aircraft.

The use of Rolls Royce RB211 engines in the Boeing 747's sold to British Airways provided work for Weybridge in making the pylons and nacelles to take them. Some machining was subcontracted to Filton and was welcome in the quiet years of the transition from BAC to BAe. Parts of another American aircraft, the Fokker F16, were subcontracted on Filton and included fuselage frames.

Under the "Buy American Act", trade between the USA and UK had been a "one way street" since at least 1945 but constant agitation by European governments for a fairer deal and access to US markets caused a relaxation of the trade barrier in the 1970's. Work on the General Dynamics **F-111** swing wing nuclear bomber resulted from a Memorandum of Understanding signed in September 1975 by the US and Her Majesty's Government. The cost of ferrying F-111's back to Sacramento, California for major overhaul and the need to reduce the out of service time of these front line aircraft were contributing factors.

Filton's involvement in the maintenance of F-111's for USAF bases in Britain was limited at first to the pyrotechnic ejector system but more than forty depot maintenance tasks are now undertaken involving almost complete dismantling and reassembly of the airframe.

Between 1978 and 1983 ninety-seven F-111's were reworked by Filton personnel either at Filton or by outside working parties and on 1 October 1984 a new four year contract was signed which involves a further minimum quantity of 120 aircraft.

A phenomenon known as **Airbus Industrie** has beaten our Colonial cousins at their own game and is now offering Britain its only opportunity to build large civil airliners. The UK, France, Germany and Spain are members of this consortium but the unwillingness of the British Government to invest in the future of British aircraft manufacturing, together with a certain reluctance to being European, has prevented Britain having a larger share of the available work.

Filton's first experience of the Airbus family of airliners has been the A310 for which it now has a steady production of details made on numerically controlled machine tools. These parts are assembled in no.3 flight shed onto wing trailing edges subcontracted from BAe Chester.

(Below)

VC10 TANKER CONVERSION (1978)

ZA141, the first of the VC10 flight refuelling tankers, on the Apron at Filton in 1980.

Between 1978 and 1985, nine Vickers VC10's were converted to aerial tankers for the RAF. Five standard aircraft originally sold to BOAC and later operated by Gulf Air were modifed to VC10 K.mk.2 while four Super VC10's built for East African Airways became VC10 K.mk.3.

Aero engines ceased to be a Bristol product when the Patchway and Rodney Works became part of Rolls Royce. Ownership of the Bristol Aeroplane Company Limited, which still existed after the formation of the British Aircraft Corporation, passed to Rolls Royce in 1966. As the Bristol Engine Division of Rolls Royce, Patchway is still building Bristol Engines notably the Pegasus vectored thrust turbofan that powers the Harrier 'Jump Jet'. The Harrier is the only operational jet aircraft in the World that can fly any way except inside out and was the brainchild of two men — one at Patchway and the other at Kingston. Dr. Hooker and his Bristol team were responsible for the revolutionary Bristol BE53 engine devised in 1957 by combining the fan of an Olympus engine on an Orpheus turbojet and using swivelling nozzles on the compressor.

Sydney Camm at Hawkers supplied the ideas for an airframe to exploit the potential of this engine. The prototype Hawker P1127 first flew in 1960 and was followed by an improved version, the Kestrel with Pegasus 5 engine, which was tested in 1961-63 by the U.S. funded Tripartate Evaluation Squadron. A supersonic development P1154 with Bristol BS100 engine was cancelled by the Wilson Government. The Harrier prototype flew in 1966 and commenced RAF service in 1969. The USA has purchased Harrier AV8A's for the Marine Corps and is now building the AV8B with McDonnell Douglas carbon fibre and metal wings.

Production of the Olympus 593 turbojet engine designed especially for Concorde ceased in the early '80's but Olympus engines are still built for industrial use. Viper engines inherited from Armstrong Siddeley were built in the mid 1960's and the small M45 engine built from 1966 for the Vohm-Focke-Wulfe VFW614 aircraft is still in service but was not a resounding success. For the Panavia Tornado, Patchway builds the Turbo-Union RB199 engine which, with the Pegasus, is the mainstay of current production. With spares orders the RB199 workload will be sustained well into the 1990's.

(Above & Below)
General Dynamics F-IIIF's from Lakenheath being reworked in the East Bay of the Aircraft Assembly Hall. Over 200 aircraft will eventually pass through the Filton shops or be covered by outside working parties.

(Above)
AIRBUS A310.
A310 at Farnborough in September 1982.

(Below)
AIRBUS A310.
Lowering the inner spar of a wing for the seventh A310 into the main assembly jig in no.3 flight shed at Filton.

Bristol is responsible for the assembly of wing trailing edges from details made at Chester and Filton. These are sent by road to Chester for completion of the wings which are then air lifted to Toulouse for final assembly.

(Above)

Bristol Pegasus engine in company with one of the AV-8S Matador versions of the Harrier now in service with the Spanish Navy. (*Rolls Royce*).

(Below)

The Stabileye remote piloted vehicle (RPV) built by Dynamics Group is the only new aircraft to be built at Filton since the formation of BAe, p.l.c. First flown in prototype form in October 1974. Over 200 flights of the mk.1 version were made.

Stabileye mk.2 fitted with a Lunenberg lens to provide a suitable radar signature was proposed as an aerial target with a 15kg payload.

Redesigned for quantity production the Stabileye mk.3 shown here at Filton can lift 25kg and can be used for battlefield reconnaissance when equipped with cameras or linescan infra-red surveillance units. The mk.3 which first flew in 1980 is catapult launched from a truck or trailer and can fly at 60-112mph for up to 2 hours on its 25hp two stroke petrol engine. It can be recovered by a conventional landing by the ground operator or by parachute.

(Top)
Tracked Rapier vehicles under construction in the Erecting Hall (MPS) where in past years Blenheims and Freighters were built.

(Above)
Tracked Rapier is a joint Stevenage/Bristol project but the FMC chassis is a bought out item.

(Below)
SEAWOLF GWS25 anti missile- missile is now in service with the Royal Navy aboard class 22 destroyers and Leander class frigates.

(Right)
SEAWOLF VL can be launched from a ship quickly and without first having to direct the launcher at the target.

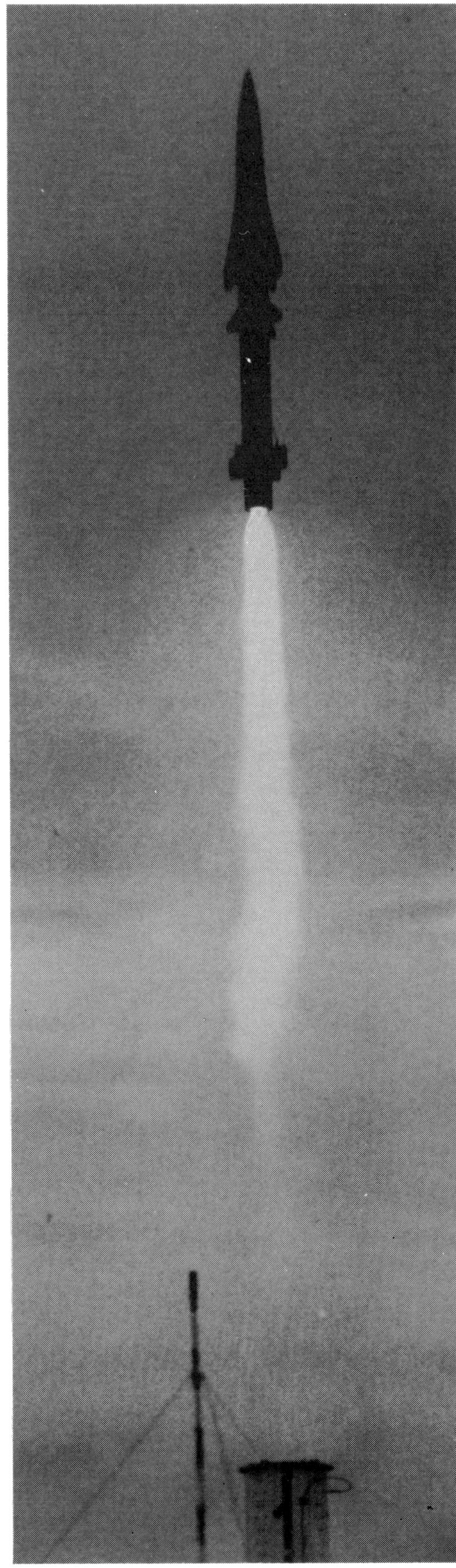

Filton Future

During the past seventy five years many aircraft manufacturers throughout the World have become only a memory but Filton has survived. Admittedly the name *Bristol* is no longer painted on the airframes but the Works is still alive and kicking. Only two other UK 'plane makers namely Avro and Blackburn which started at the beginning of British aviation have managed to stay the distance.

But what of the future? What will have happened by the year AD2010 when some historian possibly as yet unborn sits down at a word processor to compose a chronicle of ''One Hundred Years of Bristol Aerospace''?

When Sir George White founded the British and Colonial Aeroplane Company the flying machine was still very much a mystery and a tremendous gamble that paid off. Throughout the History of Filton calculated risks have been taken in producing machines not built or flown anywhere else in the World. Some like the Brabazon have been dismal failures as commercial projects but the experience gained has been put to good use by other makers if not by Bristol. In 1985 the modern jet airliner must be to us as the railway or the tram was to the populace of Britain in 1910. So what budding invention or technology is going to take Bristol into the 21st Century?

A present day reincarnation of Sir George White would recognise Space as a good source of future revenue. Europe lags behind the USA and USSR in space experience but a lucrative market awaits manufacturers of specialist equipment and companies whose technologists are of inventive mind. BAe has already responded to the challenge and at Filton a new empire is being created on a new site adjacent to the 'top works'. Included in this self contained facility is a Spacecraft Assembly Building and specialist research and development aids.

Besides exploring the frontiers of science by Government funded research there has also been, throughout the last 75 years, a recurring pattern of aircraft construction, rebuilding and servicing, and diversification into temporary sidelines.

Space vehicles could conceivably be used for long distance hauls like London to Sydney but for medium range travel to New York or sunny Spain the fixed wing aeroplane will be a familiar sight well into the next century. The effigy of Pegasus the winged horse which adorns the north wall of Filton House is appropriate in that Filton's future in aircraft seems to be as a supplier

(Below)
AIRBUS A320
Artists impression of the twin engined 150 seater A320 airliner for which Filton will contribute to the building of the high technology wings.

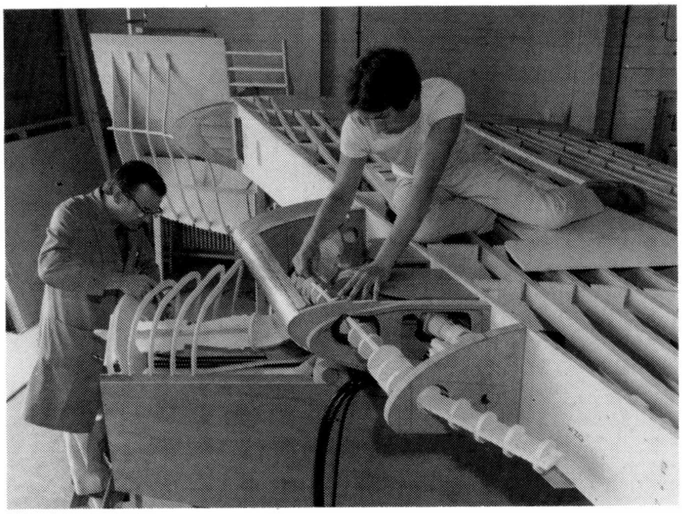

(Above)
AIRBUS A320.
Part of the wing mock-up for the new A320 under construction in the Filton 'shops in 1984.

of wings — super efficient high technology wings let it be said. Quantities are likely to be far removed from the days when 87 Beaufighters were produced every week but low volume is a fact of life for all civil aircraft makers. The 'bread and butter' of the aircraft works in the latter part of this century is likely to be wings for the new Airbus A320 and possibly other models in the Airbus family.

Rebuilding and servicing of Bristol and 'foreign' aircraft has sustained the Works after two World wars and after Concorde. It is unlikely that Filton will see more orders for VC10 tankers but the F-111 should continue. The US Government has announced its intention to keep the F-111's flying until 2010 because a substitute is not available so, for the next decade at least, Filton can look forward to further F-111's and additional tasks such as cold proof testing, wing tank resealing and avionics update.

Part of the Rodney Works has just been vacated by Rolls Royce and has been refitted as a wing shop for the special requirements of wings with integral fuel tanks.

As this book goes to press, it has been announced that from 1 May 1985 the names Aircraft Group and Dynamics Group will cease to exist. The two aspects of British Aerospace will no longer be separate entities each with its own Board of Directors but will now be organised under a ''unified Board''.

As far as Filton is concerned this may mean a slight lifting of the iron curtain that divides 'Aircraft' from 'Dynamics' but due to the differing type of product made by the two units there will always, of necessity, be some separation.

(Below)
ADVANCED SUPERSONIC TRANSPORT
One of the latest schemes for a 'super Concorde is the AST 2 devised at Filton.
It features an arrow wing planform in place of the 'ogee' wing for reduced drag, retractable silencers, and is about 50 percent longer than the production Concorde.
Before it could be built considerable work must be done to overcome the technological and political barriers.

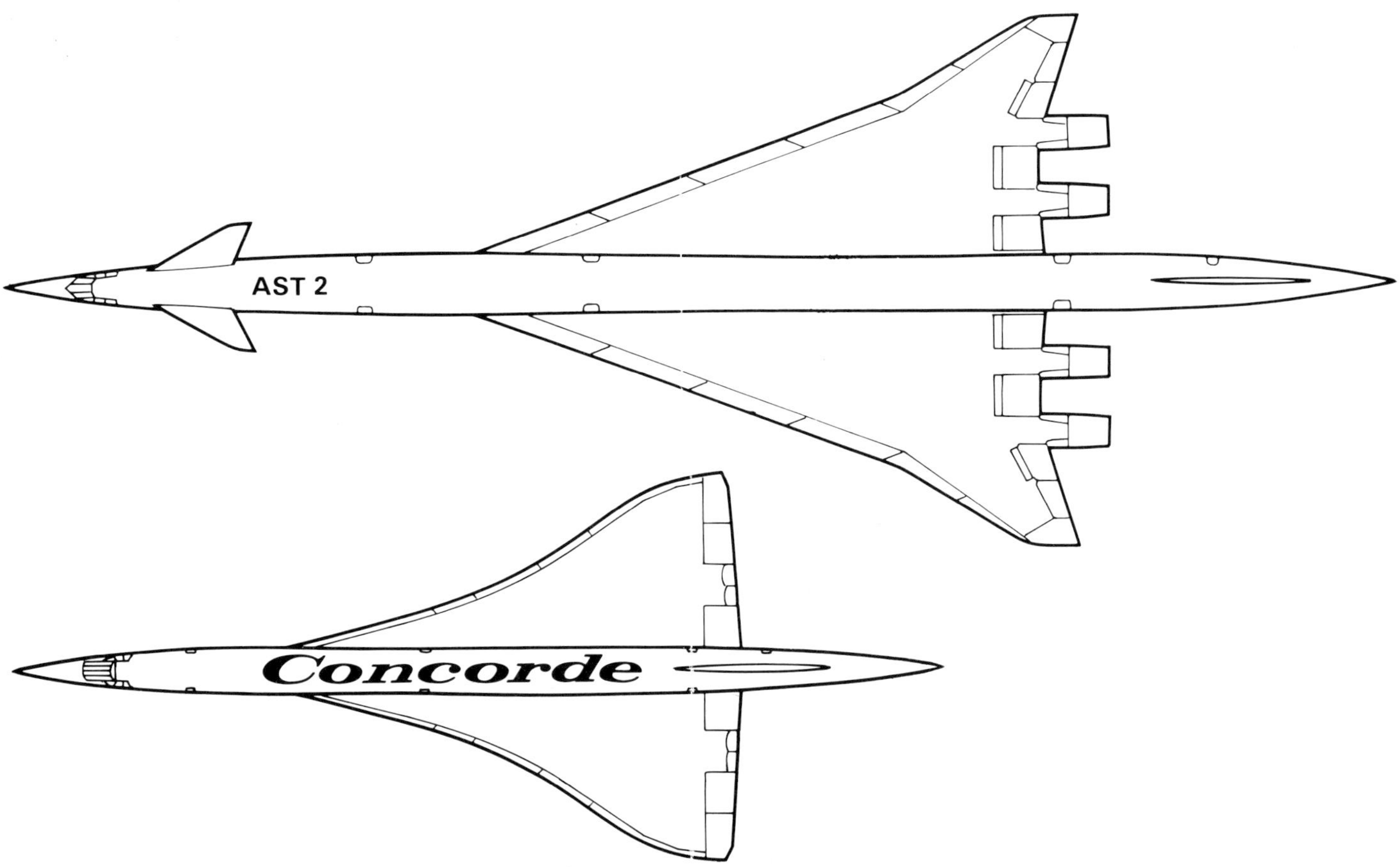

(Right)
Built by BAe Space and Communications Division at Filton, the Giotto scientific spacecraft will travel 150 million kilometers from Earth to intercept Halley's Comet when it returns in 1986 after an absence of 75 years.

(Below)
Testing of the roll out flexible panels at Filton for the solar array 'wings' of the NASA/ESA Space Telescope.

(Bottom)
Artists impression of the NASA Space Telescope fitted with solar arrays made at Filton under contract to the European Space Agency. It will be launched by space shuttle in 1986.

CHANGING FACE OF FILTON -4

A 1983 view of the Works with the new road in the foreground and the cramped old Works in contrast to the wide open spaces of the Airfield.

Bristol Aircraft Types

A complete record of the approximately 15,000 *Bristol* aircraft to be built or planned is outside the scope of this book but the following list gives a summary of the basic *Bristol* types. It should be noted, however, that there were often many marks or variants of each type.

Aircraft shown in **bold type** were built and flown or were complete airframes, sometimes for structural testing. Medium type denotes a scheme or proposed design that was not actually built although some did get as far as a wooden 'mock-up'. Names officially adopted or referred to in Company documents are shown in CAPITALS.

Type numbers were introduced in January 1924 with the type 90 and previous designs were numbered retrospectively. Numbers before type 90 are somewhat arbitrary and the student of the *Bristol* marque is advised to treat them with caution and to use the original designations to prevent confusion.

Dates shown for completed aircraft are the year of first flight, or the year of delivery in the case of structural airframes. The date quoted for proposed designs is the one given in Company literature and generally indicates the commencement of the project.

Several types were not produced at Filton but were taken up by other manufacturers. For example, a version of the type 155 Composite Aircraft was built by Armstrong Whitworth and the Beadle Company built light aircraft based upon the types 218, 219 and 220. The type 223 was not built as such but is now familiar as *Concorde.*

EARLY TYPES 1910-1914

Type No.	Official Name/Description	Engine	Date
—	**Zodiac 52B biplane**	**50hp Darracq pusher**	**1910**
—	**BIPLANE ('boxkite')**	**50/70 Gnome etc**	**1910**
—	**GLIDER**	**none**	**1910**
—	**RACING BIPLANE (no.33)**	**50hp Gnome**	**1911**
—	**TRACTOR MONOPLANE (Challenger/Low)**	**50hp Gnome**	**1911**
—	**BIPLANE T**	**50/70hp Gnome 70 Renault**	**1911**
—	**CHALLENGER-ENGLAND BIPLANE**	**60hp ENV**	**1911**
—	**PRIER MONOPLANES**	**Gnome, Anzani etc.**	**1912**
—	**GORDON ENGLAND BIPLANES**	**Clerget/Daimler/Gnome**	**1912**
—	**COANDA MONOPLANES**	**50/80hp Gnome; 70 Daimler**	**1912**
—	**COANDA BIPLANES**	**Gnome/Renault/Le Rhone**	**1913**
—	**BURNEY HYDROPED BIPLANES**	**ENV/Gnome/Canton-Unne**	**1913**
—	**BABY TRACTOR (SCOUT A)**	**Gnome/Le Rhone**	**1914**
—	**SCOUT B**	**80hp Gnome**	**1914**
—	**BE2a Royal Aircraft Factory design**		**1912**
—	**BE2b**		**1913**
—	**BE2c**		**1914**
—	**BE2d**		**1915**
—	**BE2e**		**1916**
—	**BE8**		**1914**
—	BE10		—

1914-1923 (Type numbers allocated retrospectively in 1924)

Type No.	Official Name/Description	Engine	Date
1	**SCOUT C biplane**	**80hp Gnome**	**1914**
2	**SCOUT D GNOME**	**80hp Gnome**	**1915**
3	**SCOUT D LeRHONE**	**80hp LeRhone**	**1915**
4	**SCOUT D 100 MONO**	**100hp Monosaupape-Gnome**	**1916**
5	**SCOUT D 110 CLERGET**	**110hp Clerget**	**1916**
6	**T.T.A. fighting biplane**	**two 120hp Beardmore**	**1916**
7	F3A version of T.T.A.	250hp Rolls Royce	1916
8	**S2A scout biplane**	**110hp Clerget**	**1916**
9	R2A fighting biplane	120hp Beardmore	1916
9A	R2B fighting biplane	150hp Hispano-Suiza	1916
10	**M1.A monoplane scout**	**110hp Clerget**	**1916**
11	**M1.B monoplane scout**	**Clerget or LeRhone**	**1916**
12	**F2A fighting biplane**	**190hp Rolls Royce**	**1916**
13	**MR.1 all metal fighting biplane**	**150hp Hispano-Suiza**	**1916**
14	**BRISTOL FIGHTER (F2B) mk.I & II**	**Rolls Royce Falcon**	**1917**
15	**F2B ARAB**	**200 hp Sunbeam Arab**	**1917**
16	**F2B 200 H.S.**	**200hp Hispano-Suiza**	**1918**
17	**F2B 300 H.S.**	**300hp Hispano-Suize**	**1918**
17A	**F2B 300 H.S. for Spain**	**300hp Hispano-Suiza**	**1924**
17B	**F2B 300 H.S. for Mexico**	**300hp Hispano-Suiza**	**1928**

Type No.	Official Name/Description	Engine	Date
18	SCOUT E biplane	Ricardo-Halford Cruciform	1917
19	Scout	Cruciform pusher	1917
20	**M1.C monoplane scout**	**110hp LeRhone**	**1917**
21	**SCOUT F biplane**	**200hp Sunbeam Arab**	**1918**
21A	**SCOUT F.1**	**315hp Cosmos Mercury**	**1919**
22	F2.C (Salmson)	200hp Salmson	1917
22A	F2.C (Dragonfly)	320hp ABC Dragonfly	1918
22B	F2.C (BR2)	230hp Bentley BR2	1918
23	**BADGER I two seat fighter**	**ABC Dragonfly**	**1918**
23A	**BADGER II two seat fighter**	**Cosmos Jupiter**	**1919**
23X	**BADGER X sporting/experimental**	**Siddeley Puma**	**1919**
24	**BRAEMAR I triplane day bomber**	**four 230hp Puma**	**1918**
25	**BRAEMAR II triplane day bomber**	**four 400hp Liberty 12**	**1919**
26	**PULLMAN 14 passenger triplane**	**four 400hp Liberty 12**	**1919**
—	**Parnall PANTHER**		**1919**
27	**F2B COUPE civil conversion**	**Rolls Royce Falcon**	**1919**
28	**PUMA COUPE 3 touring biplane**	**230hp Puma**	**1919**
29	**PT2S touring biplane**	**230hp Puma**	**1919**
30	**BABE I single seat sporting biplane**	**Viale**	**1919**
31	GRAMPUS I commercial biplane	500hp Siddeley Tiger	1919
32	**BULLET high performance biplane**	**450hp Cosmos Jupiter**	**1920**
32A	**BULLET modified type 32**	**450hp Cosmos Jupiter**	**1921**
32B	**BULLET modified type 32A**	**450hp Cosmos Jupiter**	**1921**
33	PULLMAN 40 passenger triplane	four Siddeley Tiger	1919
34	F2B SEAPLANE TOURER	180hp Wolseley Viper	1919
35	SHIPBOARD SEAPLANE RAF type XXI	Cosmos Jupiter	1919
36	**SEELY PUMA civil biplane**	**230hp Puma**	**1919**
37	**TRAMP triplane spares carrier**	**four 230hp Puma**	**1921**
38	AH-2 seaplane fighter 2 seats	180hp Wolseley Viper	1919
39	AH-1 seaplane fighter 1 seat	180hp Wolseley Viper	1919
40	**PUMA FIGHTER (F2B)**	**230hp Puma**	**1919**
41	BEARDMORE FLOAT SEAPLANE	120hp Beardmore	1919
42	GRAMPUS II commercial biplane	140hp RAF4a	1919
43	GRAMPUS IV eight seat biplane	four 100hp Lucifer.	1919
44	TRAMP BOAT triplane flying boat	four 230hp Puma	1919
45	SCANDINAVIAN TOURER biplane	230hp Puma	1919
46	**BABE II sporting biplane**	**Siddeley Ounce.**	**1919**
46A	**BABE III sporting biplane**	**60hp LeRhone**	**1920**
46B	**BABE MONOPLANE**	**60hp LeRhone**	**1920**
47	**PT3S three seat open tourer**	**230hp Siddeley Puma**	**1920**
48	**PUMA SEAPLANE 3 tourer**	**230hp Puma**	**1920**
49	Lucifer three seater biplane	100hp Cosmos Lucifer	1920
50	MAIL CARRIER triplane	four 400hp Liberty	1920
51	LUCIFER BOAT	Cosmos Lucifer pusher	1920
52	**MFA BULLFINCH fighter monoplane**	**Bristol Jupiter**	**1922**
53	**MFB BULLFINCH fighter biplane**	**Bristol Jupiter**	**1923**
54	MONO SEAPLANE	450hp Bristol Jupiter	1920
55	D of R.4B long distance bomber	Rolls Royce Condor	1920
56	TROOP CARRIER	520 450hp Napier Lion	1920
57	GRAMPUS V commercial biplane	two 200hp Hall-Scott	1920
58	8 SEATER LIBERTY cargo/passenger/biplane	400hp Liberty	1920
59	8 SEATER JUPITER cargo/passenger/biplane	450hp Cosmos Jupiter	1920
60	LT3 monoplane coupe 3 seater	100hp Cosmos Lucifer	1920
61	JUPITER AMPHIBIAN	Cosmos Jupiter pusher	1920
62	**10 SEATER LION**	**450hp Napier Lion**	**1921**
63	5HP monoplane — Cambridge		1921
64	Speed monoplane — Lecture		1921
65	Man powered aeroplane — Studies		1921
66	HYDROVANE BOAT	450hp Napier Lion pusher	1921
67	LION MK.II fighter recce biplane	450hp Napier Lion	1921
68	D of R Type 7A fleet gunnery spotter	450hp Napier Lion	1921
69	D of R Type 3 Adapted recce biplane	450hp Napier Lion	1921
70	D of R Type 3A recce monoplane	450hp Napier Lion	1921
71	D of R Type 9 torpedo carrying triplane	Napier Cub	1921
72	**JUPITER RACER high speed monoplane**	**Bristol Jupiter**	**1921**
73	**L3S TAXIPLANE touring biplane**	**Bristol Lucifer**	**1922**
74	26 Seater Commercial triplane	Bristol Jupiter	1921
75	**J10S commercial biplane**	**Bristol Jupiter**	**1921**
75A	**EXPRESS FREIGHT CARRIER (J10S converted)**	**Bristol Jupiter**	**1924**
76	**JUPITER FIGHTER F2B modified**	**Bristol Jupiter**	**1923**
76A	**BIFUEL JUPITER FIGHTER**	**Bristol Jupiter**	**1923**
76B	**SWEDISH JUPITER FIGHTER**	**Bristol Jupiter**	**1923**
77	**M1.D LUCIFER MONOPLANE**	**Bristol Lucifer**	**1922**

Type No.	Official Name/Description	Engine	Date
78	**BRISTOL FIGHTER TYPE C**	**Bristol Jupiter**	**1923**
79	**BRANDON Ambulance**	**Bristol Jupiter**	**1924**
80	BRISTOL FIGHTER TYPE D	Bristol Jupiter	1922
81	**PT 1923 TYPE B school machine**	**230hp Siddeley Puma**	**1923**
81A	**PUMA FIGHTER**	**230hp Puma**	**1925**
82	Coastal defence biplane	450hp Napier Lion	1923
83	**L2S Lucifer School Machine**	**100hp Bristol Lucifer**	**1923**
83A	**L2S**	**Lucifer**	**1923**
83B	**L2S**	**Lucifer**	**1926**
83C	**L2S**	**Lucifer**	**1927**
83D	**proposed twin float seaplane**	**Bristol Lucifer**	**1927**
83E	**TITAN SCHOOL MACHINE**	**Bristol Titan**	**1928**
84	**BLOODHOUND (ex Type 78)**	**Bristol Jupiter**	**1925**
84A	**BLOODHOUND**	**Jupiter IV**	**1925**
84B	**BLOODHOUND**	**Jupiter**	**1925**
85	**SEELY SUPERCHARGER (ex type 36)**	**Supercharged Jupiter**	**1923**
86	ROLLS ROYCE TOURER 2	275hp R.R. Falcon	1923
86A	ROLLS ROYCE TOURER 3	275hp R.R. Falcon	1923
87	Fleet reconnaissance biplane	Jupiter	1923
88	**BULGARIAN TOURER**	**180hp Wolseley Viper**	**1923**
88A	**IMPROVED BULGARIAN TOURER**	**180hp Wolseley Viper**	**1926**
89	**JUPITER SCHOOL MACHINE**	**Bristol Jupiter**	**1924**
89A	**JUPITER SCHOOL MACHINE**	**Bristol Jupiter**	**1926**

1924 Onwards (Given Type Numbers When Designed)

90	BERKELEY 2-seat bomber biplane	Rolls Royce Condor	1925
91	BROWNIE light monoplane	Bristol Cherub I	1924
91A	BROWNIE I	Bristol Cherub III	1924
91B	BROWNIE II	Bristol Cherub III	1926
92	LABORTORY MACHINE	Bristol Jupiter	1926
93	BOARHOUND fighter biplane	Bristol Jupiter	1924
93A	BEAVER two seat fighter biplane	Bristol Jupiter	1925
93B	BOARHOUND II fighter biplane	Bristol Jupiter	1927
94	Single seat fighter biplane	Jupiter pusher	1924
95	**BLUDGEON/BAGSHOT fighting monoplane**	**two Jupiter**	**1925**
96	**BRISTOL FIGHTER MK.III**	**275hp R.R. Falcon**	**1927**
96A	**BRISTOL FIGHTER MK.IV**	**275hp R.R. Falcon**	**1927**
97	Commercial biplane for Imperial Airways	Jupiter	1925
98	BROWNIE III light monoplane	Bristol Cherub	1925
99	**BADMINTON Sporting Biplane**	**Bristol Jupiter**	**1925**
99A	**BADMINTON rebuild of T99**	**Jupiter**	**1925**
100	Commercial biplane	two Jupiter	1925
101	**High performance fighting biplane**	**Bristol Mercury VI**	**1927**
102A	Fighter version of Badminton	Bristol Jupiter	1926
102B	Seaplane version of Badminton	Jupiter	1926
103	Single seat high speed monoplane	Bristol Mercury	1926
104	Single seat light monoplane	Bristol Cherub	1926
105	**BULLDOG prototypes**	**Bristol Jupiter**	**1927**
105A	**BULLDOG production**	**Jupiter/Mercury**	**1928**
105D	**BULLDOG for Denmark**	**Mercury**	**1931**
105J	**JAPANESE SINGLE SEAT FIGHTER (Bulldog)**	**Jupiter**	**1930**
106	General purpose biplane with DH9A wings	Jupiter	1927
107	**BULLPUP fighter**	**various Bristol**	**1928**
108	Twin Engined night bomber	two Jupiter VII	1928
—	**Armstrong Whitworth SISKIN IIIA**		**1928**
109	**LONG RANGE MACHINE**	**Jupiter VIII and XIF**	**1927**
110	Commercial Biplane 3 passengers	Bristol Titan	1928
110A	**COMMERCIAL BIPLANE 4 passengers**	**300hp Bristol Neptune**	**1928**
111A	Commercial cabin monoplane	three Jupiter	1928
111B	Commercial cabin monplane	three Titan	1928
112	Fighter monoplane F.29/27	Bristol Mercury III	1928
113	Commercial biplane	Three Jupiter XI	1928
114	Commercial biplane	one Jupiter XI	1929
114A	Commercial biplane similar to T114	one Jupiter	1929
115	Troop carrying monoplane C.16/28	three Jupiter X	1929
116	Troop carrying biplane C.16/28	three Jupiter X	1929
117	Freight carrier	two Jupiter	1929
118	**GENERAL PURPOSE BIPLANE**	**Jupiter XFA**	**1929**
118A	**G.P. BIPLANE modified T118**	**Mercury V (temporary)**	**1931**
119	Bulldog training machine	Mercury IVA	1930
120	**GENERAL PURPOSE BIPLANE**	**Mercury V/Pegasus IM3**	**1931**
121	General Purpose Bomber G.4/31	Bristol Pegasus	1931

Type No.	Official Name/Description	Engine	Date
122	General Purpose Bomber G.4/31	Bristol Pegasus	1931
123	**SINGLE SEATER FIGHTER F.7/30**	**Rolls Royce Goshawk**	**1933**
124	**BULLDOG T.M.**	**Jupiter**	**1932**
125	General purpose monoplane G.4/31	Pegasus	1931
126	General purpose monoplane G.4/31	Pegaus	1931
127	Fighter monoplane F.7/30	745hp R.R. Kestrel	1932
128	Fighter monoplane F.7/30	620hp Mercury IV.S2	1932
129	Fighter monoplane F.7/30	620hp Mercury pusher	1932
130	**Transport monoplane (Bombay prototype)**	**two Pegasus**	**1932**
130A	**BOMBAY monoplane (production)**	two Pegasus	**1935**
131	Monoplane day bomber B.9/32	two Pegasus	1933
132	Two seat fighter	Bristol Hydra	1933
133	**SINGLE SEATER FIGHTER F.7/30**	**640hp Mercury IV.S2**	**1933**
134	Mail carrying monoplane	Pegasus I	1933
135	Commercial monoplane	two Bristol Aquila	1933
136	Day bomber P.27/32	Bristol Perseus	1933
137A	14 seat commercial transport (as T130)	two Pegasus	1933
137B	Freight/passenger transport	two Pegasus	1933
138	ALTITUDE MACHINE	Pegasus	1933
138A	**ALTITUDE MACHINE (T138 revised)**	**Pegasus**	**1934**
138B	**ALTITUDE MACHINE**	**(Rolls Royce)**	**1934**
139	Freight carrier	Pegasus IIM3	1934
140	Two seat fighter F.5/33	Perseus pusher	1934
141	Three seat fighter F.22/33	two Aquila	1934
142	**BRITAIN FIRST six seat transport**	**two Mercury IV.M**	**1934**
142M	**BLENHEIM I bomber (short nose)**	**two Mercury**	**1935**
143	**PASSENGER MACHINE**	**two Aquila**	**1936**
143F	Type 143 for Finland	two Mercury	1936
144	Night bomber B.3/34 (similar to T.130)	two Perseus	1934
145A	Long range machine	two Bristol Phoenix	1935
145B	Long range machine	two Phoenix diesel	1935
146	Single seat fighter	Mercury	1936
147	Zone fighter F.9/35	Perseus	1935
147A	Zone fighter	Bristol Hercules	1935
148	**ARMY COOPERATION MACHINE**	**Mercury/Perseus**	**1935**
148A	**ARMY COOPERATION MACHINE**	**Bristol Hercules**	**1935**
148B	**ARMY COOPERATION MACHINE**	**Bristol Taurus**	**1938**
149	**BOLINGBROKE prototype (Blenheim III)**	**Hercules**	**1937**
149	**BLENHEIM IV bomber (long nose)**	**Hercules**	**1937**
149	**BOLINGBROKE (Blenheim IV made in Canada)**	**Hercules**	**1939**
150	**Torpedo bomber M.15/35**	**two Perseus**	**1935**
151	**High speed aircraft 35/35**	**Hercules**	**1935**
—	**Hawker AUDAX**		**1935**
152	**BEAUFORT torpedo bomber**	**two Taurus/Twin Wasp**	**1938**
153	Day and night fighter F.37/35	two Hercules	1936
153A	Day and night fighter F.37/35	two Aquila	1936
154	Commercial transport	four Aquila	1936
155	COMPOSITE AIRCRAFT wood/steel bomber	two Taurus	1938
156	**BEAUFIGHTER cannon armed fighter**	**two Hercules/Merlin**	**1939**
157	Bomber version of Beaufighter	two Hercules	1940
158	BEAUFIGHTER mk.III & IV slim fuselage	two Hercules/Griffon	1940
159	Heavy bomber B.1/39	four Hercules (mock up)	1941
160	**BISLEY (prototypes)**	**two Mercury**	**1940**
160	**BLENHEIM V (production-Rootes)**	**two Mercury**	**1940**
161	BEAUMONT bomber version of T.156	two Hercules/Merlin	1940
162	BEAUMONT	two Hercules (mock up)	1940
163	**BUCKINGHAM medium bomber**	**two Bristol Centaurus**	**1943**
164	**BRIGAND torpedo fighter bomber**	**two Centaurus**	**1944**
165	BRIGAND MK.II dual control trainer	two Centaurus	1944
166	**BUCKMASTER trainer version of T.163**	**two Centaurus**	**1945**
—	**Hawker TEMPEST II**	**Centurus**	**1944**
167	**BRABAZON 1 mk.1 & 2 airliner**	**eight Centaurus**	**1950**
168	100 TON BOMBER	eight Centaurus	1944
169	BUCKINGHAM P.R. photo-recce	two Centaurus	1945
170	**FREIGHTER/WAYFARER**	**two Hercules**	**1946**
171	**SYCAMORE helicopter**	**Wasp/Leonides**	**1947**
172	High speed long range bomber OR.230	4/6 turbojets	1946
173	**Tandem rotor helicopter (ROTOCOACH)**	**two Alvis Leonides**	**1953**
174	Research aircraft		1947
175	**BRITANNIA airliner**	**four Bristol Proteus**	**1952**
176	Scale model research aircraft E.8/47	Rolls Royce Avon	1948
177	Sub sonic fighter		1949
178	Rocket fighter F.124T		1951

Type No.	Official Name/Description	Engine	Date
179	170 Freighter replacement	two Hercules	1951
179A	170 Freighter replacement	two Hercules	1952
179B	170 Freighter replacement	two Centaurus	1954
180	Supersonic fighter	two Bristol Olympus	1953
181	Twin rotor 20/50 seat helicopter	two Siddeley Mamba	1952
182	RED RAPIER expendable bomber	Bristol Saturn	1952
182R	**RED RAPIER retrievable prototype**	**Bristol Saturn**	**1953**
183	Variable sweepback supersonic fighter	R.R. Nene	1952
184	Delta wing research aircraft	R.R. Nene	1952
185	Rocket powered research aircraft	Spectre	1952
186	Long range low level bomber OR.324		1952
187	Britannia replacement	four Bristol Orion	1953
188	**High speed research aircraft**	**D.H. Gyron Junior**	**1961**
188N	H.S. research aircraft naval version		1955
189	Marine Reconnaissance Aircraft 175 type	Napier Nomad	1955
190	Ultra light helicopter HR.144	Tip jets	1954
191	**Twin rotor naval helicopter (HP146)**	**Leonides/Gazelle**	**1954**
192	**BELVEDERE-RAF helicopter**	**Napier Gazelle**	**1960**
193	Twin rotor anti-submarine helicopter	Napier Gazelle	1954
194	Twin rotor civil helicopter	Gnome	1955
195	Transport aircraft with Britannia wings	Bristol Proteus	1955
196	Unmanned bomber version of T.188	Bristol BE36	1955
197	Boundary layer control civil transport		1954
198A	Supersonic Transport (alloy airframe)	Bristol Olympus	1956
198B	S.S.T. as T.198A but 3 nacelles	Bristol Olympus	1956
198S	Supersonic Transport (steel airframe)	Bristol Olympus	1956
199	Convertiplane	four R.R. Tynes	1956
200	Short/medium range BEA transport	turbojet	1956
201	Long range BOAC transport as T.200		1956
202	Medium range low altitude bomber	two Olympus	1956
203	Sycamore replacement helicopter	Gnome	1957
204	Supersonic Tactical Strike reconnaissance aircraft	two Olympus	1957
204F	Supersonic fighter OR329	two Olympus	1957
205	Short/medium range transport	body mounted engines	1958
206	N.A.T.O. maritime reconnaissance aircraft	two R.R. Tynes	1958
207	N.A.T.O. MRA aircraft	2 Mamba and 2-BE53	1958
208	V/STOL aircraft GOR351		1958
209	V/STOL aircraft fan lift GOR351		1958
210	V/STOL aircraft jet lift GOR351		1958
211	Short range jet passenger aircraft	wing mounted engines	1958
212	Strategic transport military version		1959
—	Stand off bomb and parent aircraft		1958
213	Mach 3 Supersonic Transport		1959
214	Single rotor helicopter	two Gnome turbines	1959
215	Slender Delta Research aircraft		1959
216	Freighter car ferry	two R.R. Dart	1959
217	V/STOL reconnaissance aircraft OR345	Bristol BE53	1959
218	Light communications aircraft	two Continental 10-470	1959
219	Executive aircraft	Continental 10-470	1959
220	Executive aircraft	two Continental 10-470	1959
221	**Fairey FD.2 conversion to ogee wing**	**Rolls Royce Avon**	**1960**
222	Lockheed C130 with boundary layer control	four R.R. Tyne	1961
223	Mach 2.2 Supersonic Transport	four Olympus	1961
224	V/STOL transport for NATO	two BS Pegasus plus eight R.R. RB175	1962
225	STOL aircraft GOR351	four R.R. RB168	1962
225	STOL aircraft GOR357 marine reconnaissance	four R.R. RB168	1962

Bristol Aero Engines

A history of *Bristol* aircraft achievement would not be complete without recognition of the important part played by the Bristol Engine works at Patchway. The following summary gives only the main engine classifications and as with the airframes there were often many variants of individual engine types.

Bold type denotes an engine that was built and at least test run while those in medium type were partially built but then cancelled before completion. Dates shown are as near as possible to the year that an engine was first run.

Cosmos Engines.

Mercury	**14 cylinder radial**	**315hp**	**1917**
Jupiter	**9 cylinder radial**	**450-500hp**	**1918**
Lucifer	**3 cylinder inverted 'Y'**	**290-595hp**	**1919**

Bristol Poppet Valve Engines.

Jupiter	**9 cylinder radial**	**290-595hp**	**1920**
Cherub	**2 cylinder flat twin**	**18-36hp**	**1922**
Lucifer	**3 cylinder inverted 'Y'**	**118-140hp**	**1923**
Mercury	**9 cylinder radial**	**400-1065hp**	**1926**
Orion	**9 cylinder radial**	**485hp**	**1926**
Titan	**5 cylinder radial**	**200/240hp**	**1927**
Neptune	**7 cylinder radial**	**300hp**	**1929**
Pegasus	**9 cylinder radial**	**570-1030hp**	**1932**
Phoenix	**9 cylinder compression ignition**	**485hp**	**1932**
Draco	***Pegasus* with direct petrol injection**	**590hp**	**1932**
Hydra	**16 cylinder, 2 row radial**	**750hp**	**1933**

Bristol Sleeve Valve Engines.

Perseus	**9 cylinder radial**	**580hp**	**1932**
Aquila	**9 cylinder radial**	**460-750hp**	**1934**
Hercules	**14 cylinder, 2 row radial**	**1275-2200hp**	**1935**
Taurus	**14 cylinder, 2 row radial**	**1050hp**	**1936**
Centaurus	**18 cylinder, 2 row radial**	**1800-3300hp**	**1938**
Orion	18 cylinder, 2 row radial	3750-4000hp	1944

Bristol Gas Turbines.

Theseus	**Free turbine turo-prop**	**2200hp**	**1946**
Proteus	**Free turbine turbo-prop**	**3500-4700hp**	**1949**
BE10 Olympus	**Two spool turbojet**	**9750-40000lb. thrust.**	**1950**
BE22 Saturn	Expendable turbojet	3750lb. thrust.	1952
BE25 Orion	**Two spool constant power turbo-prop.**	**5050hp**	**1955**
BE26 Orpheus	**Light-weight turbojet**	**3285-8170lb.**	**1955**
BE47	**Turbojet version of *Orion***	**8000lb**	**1956**
BE53 Pegasus	**Vectored thrust turbo fan**	**11000-21500lb**	**1957**
BE59	Ducted fan lift engine	800lb	1958
BS75	**Bypass turbojet**	**7000-8000lb**	**1962**
BS100	**Vect. thrust turbofan (plenum chamber burning)**	**36000lb.**	**1964**
M45H	**Turbonfan**	**7600 lb.**	**1970**
RB199	**3 spool turbofan**	**8000-14000lb.**	**1971**
RB401	**Turbofan**	**5000lb.**	**1975**
RJ500	**Turbofan (V2500)**	**16000lb.**	**1983**

Bristol Ramjets.

Thor	**16 inch ramjet for *Bloodhound***		**1954**
Odin	**Ramjet for *Sea Dart***		

POSTSCRIPT

When the Aircraft and Dynamics activities in Bristol are viewed as a whole, Filton forms the largest site within British Aerospace. Add to these two the former Bristol Engine Division at Patchway (now Rolls Royce, Bristol) and then Bristol becomes the largest aerospace manufacturing unit in the United Kingdom. With a combined workforce approaching 20,000 the Filton Airfield has the largest concentration of people on a single aerospace site anywhere in the World. Head counting is admittedly not the complete criteria for success in the age of modern technology and robots but it still represents phenominal growth since the days in 1910 when a small team of craftsmen made biplanes in two iron sheds.

In recent years, Filton and Patchway, with a little help from our friends, has set the pace for the aircraft industry in the rest of the World with the two most advanced aircraft to be built so far — the Bristol Olympus engined BAC/Aerospatiale Concorde (largely based on the Bristol type 223) and the Bristol Pegasus engined Hawker Harrier ''Jump jet''.

Enough said?